ONE DAY IN YOUR HOUSE

Copyright © 2022 by: WATCHMAIDENS

ISBN-13: 978-118-102-023-0

Published by Watchmaidens Ministry

All rights reserved.

No portion of this book may be used without the written permission of the publisher, with the exception of brief excerpts in magazines, articles, reviews, etc.

For further information or permission

Address:

WATCHMAIDENS MINISTRY INTERNATIONAL
Plot 289, D Close. 33/331 Road, Egbeda,
Ipaja, Lagos.

Email: watchmaidensint@gmail.com

Telephone: +2349076566211, +2348181006070, +2348183134470

All Scripture quotations are from the King James, Amplified, Passion Translation, Message Bible, New Living Translation, New American Standard Bible, New King James Version, Good News Translation and Holman Christian Standard Bible versions of the Bible.

CONTENT

ACKNOWLEDGMENT _____ 6

INTRODUCTION _____ 8

CHAPTER ONE – *The House of God* _____ 12
- The House of Impartation..................18
- The House of Transformation.............. 19
- The Christian Practice....................22
- Prayer Point..............................25

CHAPTER TWO – *The House of God in the Wilderness* _____ 26
- The TABERNACLE; the Tent of Meeting.................29
- 1. The Outer Court....................................31
- 2. The Holy Place..................................... 33
- 3. The Most Holy Place; The Holy of Holies......... 35
- The Tabernacle Implications.........................37
- Prayer Point..39

CHAPTER THREE – *The Keepers of the Tabernacle* _____ 40
- The Levites...40
- The Descendants of Levi..............................42
- Prayer Point...45

CHAPTER FOUR – *The Rebellion of Korah* _____ 46
- The Children of Korah............................ 51
- The Sons of Korah in The Psalms..................54
- Lessons About the Sons of Korah.................. 59
- Prayer Point.....................................62

CHAPTER FIVE – *The Desire of David for the House of God* _____ 63
- Factors that determine the Presence of God...... 65
- Prayer Point.....................................72

CHAPTER SIX – *The Manifest Presence of God* _____ 73

Accessing the Presence of God via Brokenness....79
Prayer Point..86
CHAPTER SEVEN - *The Civilization of Light in His Presence* 87

The Standard of God Revealed in Light................92
Journey from Flesh to Spirit................................95
Profiting from the Spirit Realm.......................... 98
Prayer Point..101
CHAPTER EIGHT - *Dwelling in His Light* 102

Heeding God's Call..108
Prayer Point..111
CHAPTER NINE - *The Economy of Sound in His Presence* 112

Prayer Point..120
CHAPTER TEN - *Christ Revealed in His Presence* 121

The Preeminence of Jesus the Christ................126
Prayer Point..133
CHAPTER ELEVEN - *Our Walk with Christ* 134

Christ the Administrator................................. 143
Prayer Point..146
CHAPTER TWELVE - *His Presence; A Place of Dealings* 147

Discipline Versus Appetite............................... 150
Prayer Point.. 159
CHAPTER THIRTEEN - *An Environment; Not a Location* 160

Accessing God's Environment........................166
The Government of His Presence 168
Prayer Point..171
CHAPTER FOURTEEN - *In His Presence* 172

Daily Expectation of God's Presence................176

   Practicing Stillness..................................178
   The Tabernacle in Practice.....................180
   Prayer Point..186
CHAPTER FIFTEEN – *Practice His Presence* — 187
   How to Practice His Presence.................188
   Prayer Points...196
CONCLUSION – *The devil's Battle Cry* — 197
   Balak and Balaam..................................198
ABOUT THE AUTHOR — 206

ACKNOWLEDGMENT

We acknowledge our Heavenly Father for making us vessels through which the world can touch Him.

Psalm 84:1-12

1. How amiable [are] thy tabernacles, O LORD of hosts!
2. My soul longeth, yea, even fainteth for the courts of the LORD: my heart and my flesh crieth out for the living God.
3. Yea, the sparrow hath found an house, and the swallow a nest for herself, where she may lay her young, [even] thine altars, O LORD of hosts, my King, and my God.
4. Blessed [are] they that dwell in thy house: they will be still praising thee. Selah.
5. Blessed [is] the man whose strength [is] in thee; in whose heart [are] the ways [of them].
6. [Who] passing through the valley of Baca make it a well; the rain also filleth the pools.
7. They go from strength to strength, [every one of them] in Zion appeareth before God.
8. O LORD God of hosts, hear my prayer: give ear, O God of Jacob. Selah.
9. Behold, O God our shield, and look upon the face of thine anointed.
10. For a day in thy courts [is] better than a thousand. I had rather be a doorkeeper in the house of my God, than to dwell in the tents of wickedness.
11. For the LORD God [is] a sun and shield: the LORD will give grace and glory: no good [thing] will he withhold from them that walk uprightly.
12. O LORD of hosts, blessed [is] the man that trusteth in thee. (KJV)

INTRODUCTION

Man, unlike any other of God's creation, is uniquely created to experience God. Not knowing God and His capacity for intimacy, is tantamount to denying our fundamental purpose in life. Back in the Garden of Eden, before man's fall, God did not come down in the cool of the day to fellowship with the animals and plants. He came down to fellowship with Adam and Eve.

Genesis 3:8a
And they heard the sound of the Lord God walking in the garden in the cool of the day . . . (AMP)

Amongst all of God's creation, man is the only creature implanted with spiritual yearnings and aspirations, leading him to prayer and worship.

Wherever man is found, he is engaged in some sort of worship. Something within him lifts itself in response to something within, the Creator, in whose image and likeness man was formed.

Genesis 1:27

So God created man in His own image, in the image and likeness of God He created him; male and female He created them. (AMP)

Consider the young eagle that is born to fly; a natural yearning within its breasts, leads it to mount up on wings and ascend into the sky with a thousand feet of clean air beneath its wings. The eagle might occasionally walk on the ground or perch on a tree but everything about it is designed to fly in the air. Even when its wings are clipped and it cannot fly, it still would have the burning desire to mount up on wings.

Such is the plight of humanity. We are born to ascend into the very presence of God where we belong; deep calling unto deep (Psalm 42:7). The greatest discovery of humanity, especially for the hungry heart, is the discovery of the manifest, conscious presence of God. In the deep recesses of a man's heart lies an overwhelming yearning towards the Creator. Unless and until that desire is fully met, the human heart remains restless. St Augustine, the Bishop of Hippo, captured the essence of his desire in his confession thus; *"thou has created us for thyself and we are restless until we rest fully in thee".* God created man to express His pleasure and fellowship.

Revelation 4:11
Thou art worthy, O Lord, to receive glory and honour and power: for thou hast created all things, and for thy pleasure they are and were created. (KJV)

Nothing in, or of this world, measures up to the simple pleasure of experiencing the presence of God. Our whole purpose as created beings is to utilize our time, delighting in the manifest presence of our Creator. The presence of God is so indescribable that some, in trying to explain it, are lost for words. Only those with personal and intimate knowledge of God's presence, can understand this. Some things simply soar above explanation and human understanding, and this is one of them.

Intimacy with the Creator, separates man from every other creature. The whole purpose of God, bringing us into right relationship with Him, is for us to come into conscious relationship with Him. He wants us to be conscious of Him, as He is of us.

May God enable us in our spiritual journey to experience all that He has in store for us and may we come away from reading this book, with a fresh desire to live in the manifest, conscious presence of God.

One day in Your house Lord is better than a thousand elsewhere. I would rather be a gatekeeper in the house of my God than to live in the tents of the wicked.

"Just One Passion, One Purpose
Is To Know You More And More
When I Know You, I Will Find Me.
No Life Outside You; No One Beside You
Let Me Know You More And More
When I Know You, I Will Find Me."

----- *Dunsin Oyekan*

CHAPTER ONE

The House of God

Psalm 84:1-2

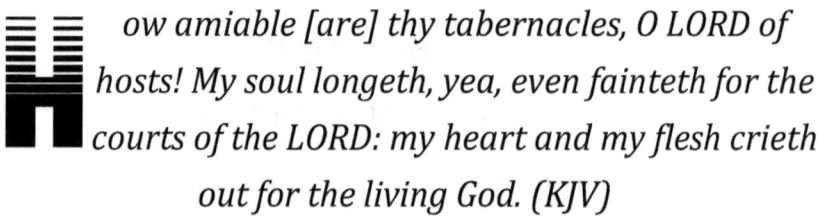

ow amiable [are] thy tabernacles, O LORD of hosts! My soul longeth, yea, even fainteth for the courts of the LORD: my heart and my flesh crieth out for the living God. (KJV)

In Europe, there are lots of breathtaking cathedrals that are so overwhelmingly beautiful. Many were built when architecture was used as a means of worshipping God. An elderly lady went on a tour in one of the greatest cathedrals in Europe, and a tour guide was showing her the great architectural designs, paintings, great glass windows and vivid scenes of the Bible that surrounded the building. He talked about the fact that the artworks in the cathedral were some of the most priced works by great masters of art. Finally, the tour ended and the little lady looked at the tour guide and told him she wasn't impressed by all he showed her. She asked him, *"young man how many souls have been saved in this place?"* The man was shocked because he had never been asked such a question on the tour of the cathedral before.

He replied thus, *"Madam, this is a cathedral, not a chapel"*. How sad is the deadness of the cathedrals in Europe; mighty edifices with little or no real Kingdom work being done in them. It is only the presence of the Almighty God that makes a house *the house of God*. The first place that was called the house of God in the Bible was not a building. Jacob met with God in that place, when he was running away from his brother Esau.

Genesis 28:16-19

16. And Jacob awaked out of his sleep, and he said, Surely the LORD is in this place; and I knew [it] not.

> *17. And he was afraid, and said, How dreadful [is] this place! this [is] none other but the house of God, and this [is] the gate of heaven.*
> *18. And Jacob rose up early in the morning, and took the stone that he had put [for] his pillows, and set it up [for] a pillar, and poured oil upon the top of it.*
> *19. And he called the name of that place Bethel: but the name of that city [was called] Luz at the first. (KJV)*

Jacob called the place, *"the house of God"*, the gate of heaven; for the house of God is His dwelling place.

> *This is the ladder in the Spirit,*
> *My gateway to the heavens.*
> *The connection to the Father,*
> *My worship brings me face to face.*
> *I worship the One who sits upon the throne…*
> - Dunsin Oyekan

Some people go to the house of God only three times in their lifetime. The first time, when water is thrown on them; their christening. The second time is when rice is thrown on them; their wedding. And the third time is when dirt is thrown on them; their burial. This is as far as it goes with millions of people worldwide. However, the bible says that they go from strength to strength, increasing in victorious power, each of them that appears before the Lord in Zion (Psalm 84:7). No wonder a vast majority of the world are sick, weak, powerless and dying.

It is always a privilege to be in God's house, and in His presence. There is never a wasted moment in the presence of the Lord. You can have wasted moments before men, but never before God.

The Bible says that the Lord is Spirit; and where the Spirit of the Lord is, there is liberty (2 Corinthians 3:17). Wherever God is, there He expresses Himself in doing what is good and changing lives.

Zephaniah 3:17
The LORD your God in your midst, The Mighty One, will save; He will rejoice over you with gladness, He will quiet you with His love, He will rejoice over you with singing."(NKJV)

You have to trust and understand the value of God's presence. One moment, just one moment in His presence, can truly change your life. No wonder the psalmist declared in Psalm 84;

Psalm 84:1-4

1. How lovely is Your tabernacle, O LORD of hosts!
2. My soul longs, yes, even faints For the courts of the LORD; My heart and my flesh cry out for the living God.
3. Even the sparrow has found a home, And the swallow a nest for herself, Where she may lay her young-- Even Your altars, O LORD of hosts, My King and my God.
4. Blessed are those who dwell in Your house; They will still be praising You. Selah (NKJV)

We must never be casual about the house of God; never be casual about the Word of God; never be casual about an atmosphere where the Spirit of God has been allowed to be Himself, and find expression in the lives of men. There is no telling how far God is able to lift, build, change and transform lives in such a place.

1 Chronicles 29:11-12

11. Thine, O LORD, [is] the greatness, and the power, and the glory, and the victory, and the majesty: for all [that is] in the heaven and in the earth [is thine]; thine [is] the kingdom, O LORD, and thou art exalted as head above all.

12. Both riches and honour [come] of thee, and thou reignest over all; and in thine hand [is] power and might; and in thine hand [it is] to make great, and to give strength unto all. (KJV)

The house of God is not a cinema or an entertainment house; it is far beyond being an ordinary lecture room or a place of disseminating information; it is the gate of heaven.

Many things happen when you are in the presence of the Lord. Oh! the great possibilities in His presence. There are healings, miracles, signs and wonders, as the Word of God comes to deconstruct faulty belief systems. In a moment, in a twinkling of an eye, an ideology you have submitted to for decades, which has sponsored negative cycles, patterns, limitations, embargoes, failures and defeat in your life, fizzles away. One Word accurately explained from the Bible can bring you great deliverance, and your life will be so transformed and impacted that you will never remain the same again.

The House of Impartation

The house of God is a house of impartation. The word "impartation" is referred to, as the transference of spiritual possibilities. This occurs very regularly while we are seated in a service in God's house. Beyond the man of God who is speaking, teaching or preaching, there is The God who works constantly in the midst of His people.

Isaiah 64:4

For from of old no one has heard nor perceived by the ear, nor has the eye seen a God besides You, Who works and shows Himself active on behalf of him who [earnestly] waits for Him. (AMP)

He moves from seat to seat, row to row, gallery to gallery, hall to hall, searching the intents of the hearts, the hunger and expectation of man, and then coordinating the words that come to save, heal, deliver and destroy strongholds. While you are seated in His house, you will be amazed to know the kind of ascendance you are having in the spirit. Physically, you are seated, but in the realm of the spirit, there is an elevation and transformation happening to you. It is the law of transformation.

The House of Transformation

The Bible says that every time you truly behold Him, you experience a change of level.

2 Corinthians 3:18

But we all, with open face beholding as in a glass the glory of the Lord, are changed into the same image from glory to glory, [even] as by the Spirit of the Lord.

(KJV)

The Word of God does not just tell you who God is and what God can do, it brings you into that experience. Lest we get used to just coming to His house for a church program, it is dangerous to be casual in God's presence. Jacob said, *"The Lord was in this place and I knew it not"*. As powerful as His presence is, a lack of hunger and expectation can make it seem as if God is absent.

Don't ever say I am *just* coming to church. Don't ever say I am *just* coming to hear a man of God, or to honor a meeting that is organized by a popular ministry. It is more than that, it is an encounter of a life time. The house of God is the place of encounters. I hope you know that it is the presence of God that makes heaven to be *heaven;* not the angels, nor the four creatures, twenty-four elders, archangels, nor the Cherubim or Seraphim. The same presence of God that we seek is also sought after by the hosts of heaven.

Consequently, hell is what it is because there is no manifestation of the conscious presence of God there. God's presence is the life-giving factor in heaven. Beyond the healings, deliverances and people falling under the power of the anointing, it is His presence that makes us become like Christ. This is why we gather and gather, again and again, and learn and listen, again and again to His Word.

Psalm 84:10
For a day in thy courts [is] better than a thousand. I had rather be a doorkeeper in the house of my God, than to dwell in the tents of wickedness. (KJV)

If one day in His house can accomplish so much, how much more will dwelling in His manifest presence permanently do?

Psalm 91:1

HE WHO dwells in the secret place of the Most High shall remain stable and fixed under the shadow of the Almighty [Whose power no foe can withstand]. (AMP)

The promise of Psalm 91:1 is for 'he who dwells', not he who only visits the secret place of the Most High. The grace to move from being mere visitors, to dwelling permanently in God's presence is released upon us now in the Name of Jesus.

Hebrews 10:22-25

22. Let us draw near with a true heart in full assurance of faith, having our hearts sprinkled from an evil conscience, and our bodies washed with pure water.
23. Let us hold fast the profession of [our] faith without wavering; (for he [is] faithful that promised;)
24. And let us consider one another to provoke unto love and to good works:
25. Not forsaking the assembling of ourselves together, as the manner of some [is]; but exhorting [one

> *another]: and so much the more, as ye see the day approaching. (KJV)*

The above verses of the Scriptures imply that dwelling in God's presence as we fellowship with one another, is a necessity. When going to church becomes a problem, something is wrong. When the circle of believers become too dull for us to associate with, many excuses will be given.

The Christian Practice

From the very beginning of Christianity, it has been a regular practice for believers to come together to worship, pray, reminisce, anticipate, search the Scriptures, sing holy hymns, and testify.

> **Acts 4:23**
> *And being let go, they went **to their own company**, and reported all that the chief priests and elders had said unto them. (KJV)*

People always go to their own company, and it is perfectly normal. Those who rear sheep know that it is only the sick sheep that does not like the flock. It wanders off by itself into the bush. Only the healthy ones stay with the flock.

Jesus Christ went to the synagogue regularly. Though He did not agree with much that He found there, He went because he had to be in the company of people who were at least, essentially worshipping God.

> ***Matthew 18:20***
> *For where two or three are gathered together in My name, I am there in the midst of them." (NKJV)*

During the week, we go to school, we work, we buy, we sell, and we interact with different people with different backgrounds and belief systems. We drive our cars and do a lot of things all week long under pressure. In the midst of it all however, we have it at the back of our minds that there exists a company of people who think as we think, whose hearts are like our hearts, who love what we love, and who are our people with faces we can recognize. We know who they are, and we like to be with them.

As believers, don't you think this is reason enough for us to go to church every time we can? Brethren we need each other.

Deuteronomy 32:30 (Paraphrase)
... one have chased a thousand, and two put ten thousand to flight, (AMP)

Usually, when a Christian loses his love for the company of the saints, he begins to rationalize. He casts aspersion on the pastor, the choir and how they minister, the unfriendliness of the people, the hypocrites in the church, or even the church building and its location. But if he understands that these people are his own people, and that he also is not perfect, he will love them, knowing that there is corporate delight in the presence of God.

Let us draw near to GOD
Let us hold fast our Christian profession
Let us consider one another and be responsible to helping each other.
Let us not forsake the assembly of ourselves together.
For the sweetest place in the world is the assembly of the saints.

Thank God for the freedom in our land, where there is no secret police listening to what we say, ready to arrest us and condemn us because we dare to talk about God, to a people that want to hear about Him.

Let us not sell it out or neglect it. We must take advantage of our freedom to worship God among the people of God. Like the Psalmist, let us declare;

Psalm 27:4
One [thing] have I desired of the LORD, that will I seek after; that I may dwell in the house of the LORD all the days of my life, to behold the beauty of the LORD, and to enquire in his temple. (KJV)

This was David's desire, which made him a man after God's own heart. May this be our hearts' desire in Jesus' Mighty Name.

Prayer Point

Father in the Name of Jesus, we thank You for Your Word in due season. Help us never to be wary of Your house, but to continually catch fresh revelation of it as Your dwelling place, and our place of divine encounters. In Jesus' Mighty Name, Amen.

CHAPTER TWO

The House of God in the Wilderness

Genesis 1:31

nd God saw every thing that he had made, and, behold, [it was] very good. And the evening and the morning were the sixth day. *(KJV)*

In the beginning, God created Adam and Eve, placing them in the beautiful Garden, east of Eden. And God said 'it is good', meaning that all creation was in absolute harmony with God and fulfilling its ordained purpose. Keep in mind that whatever God created, He did for His purpose and pleasure.

Revelation 4:11

Thou art worthy, O Lord, to receive glory and honour and power: for thou hast created all things, and for thy pleasure they are and were created. (KJV)

To entertain the idea that God would do anything without a purpose, is to misunderstand completely, the nature of God. Adam and Eve were created to live perpetually in the presence of God. In the cool of the day, God came down and walked with them in the Garden of Eden, where they offered their reverence and adoration. This was their unique purpose, shared by nothing else in all of God's creation.

God desires to be near His people, and this is made evident in the magnificent story of the redemption, that unfolds from the book of Genesis to Revelation. God began to draw near His people in a unique way, following their deliverance from Egyptian slavery and bondage.

They were delivered from slavery and oppression through series of plagues, followed by the parting of the Red sea, so they could walk across on dry ground (Psalm 136:13). In His desire to be near His people, God decided to create a space where he could dwell with them. He sought a special place which He called *"the tent of meeting";* a place of closeness because God loved His people.

A man's experience with God is usually in accordance to his location; just as in the planetary orbit. The condition of the planets are consistent with, and in accordance to their relationship with the sun. The closer planets are warmer, while those further away from the sun, are colder. Similarly, your experience as a believer is based on your distance from His presence.

Exodus 25:8-9

8. And let them make me a sanctuary; that I may dwell among them.

9. According to all that I shew thee, [after] the pattern of the tabernacle, and the pattern of all the instruments thereof, even so shall ye make [it]. (KJV)

Exodus 29:43-46

43. And there I will meet with the children of Israel, and [the tabernacle] shall be sanctified by my glory.

> *44. And I will sanctify the tabernacle of the congregation, and the altar: I will sanctify also both Aaron and his sons, to minister to me in the priest's office.*
> *45. And I will dwell among the children of Israel, and will be their God.*
> *46. And they shall know that I [am] the LORD their God, that brought them forth out of the land of Egypt, that I may dwell among them: I [am] the LORD their God.*
> *(KJV)*

The TABERNACLE; the Tent of Meeting.

The word *"tabernacle"* means the dwelling place or tent; the sanctuary or the tent of testimony. The tabernacle was a portable and moveable sanctuary that accomplished two goals;

1. It allowed God's people to draw near and worship Him, and;

2. It clarified and established the magnitude of God's holiness.

As we consider God's desire to dwell with His people, we must ponder deeply on the nature of God. He existed before time began; He is transcendent, dwelling in eternity, without beginning or end. He is self-sufficient and self-existent. He is separate, holy, powerful and sovereign. Therefore, for us to draw near and worship Him, we must recognize that above all, God is Lord and He is Spirit.

The tabernacle building helps us recognize this truth because of its very design. We must worship God in reverential fear and awe, embracing the free gift of His permission for us to come freely in His presence.

Song of Solomon 2:10
My lover has arrived and he's speaking to me! Get up, my dear friend, fair and beautiful lover--come to me!
(MSG)

The tabernacle therefore provides a visual image of these two characteristics of God;
1. His holiness.
2. His love for us.

Chapter Two – The House of God in the Wilderness

THE TABERNACLE OF MOSES (EXODUS 35-40)

Image downloaded from Growing Christian Resources

The tabernacle is made up of three major parts which we will consider in detail as follows:
1. The Outer Court.
2. The Holy Place.
3. The Most Holy Place (Holy of Holies)

1. The Outer Court

* **The Wall**: This is the wall or border that surrounds the tabernacle and it is made of linen curtain.

* **The East Gate:** This is also called the door, and the only gate that leads into the tabernacle.

* **The Brazen Altar:** This is also known as the place of sacrifice. The brazen altar of burnt offerings is the place where animals were sacrificed. Only the priests made sacrifices for two purposes namely:
1. for the atonement of sin.
2. for thanksgiving, praise and worship to God.

* **The Brazen Laver:** This is also known as the place of washing. As we move forward through the tabernacle, past the brazen altar, we come to the brazen laver for cleansing. Here, the priests cleanse themselves daily before going into God's presence.

All the above are outside, under the natural light of the sun.

2. The Holy Place

The Holy place is tent-like, covered with several layers of fine linen and waterproof animal skin. Only a priest could enter the holy place. Inside the holy place are the following:

* **The Table and the Shew Bread:** This is also known as the bread of presence or the show bread. The table with the bread of presence, consists of twelve loaves of bread placed on the table as an offering to God.

* **The Lampstand:** This is also referred to as the golden candlesticks. The golden lampstand or the menorah is another element in the holy place. The lampstand provided light to the area, and represented the light of God's presence. While the outer court depended on the natural light of the sun, the holy place was lit by the golden lampstand.

* **The Golden Altar of Incense:** The third and central element in the holy place, was the altar of incense. It was capable of ushering anyone into the presence of God. Here, the power of intercession was experienced.

The holy incense burned continually upon the coals of the altar.

Exodus 30:6-8

6. And thou shalt put it before the vail that [is] by the ark of the testimony, before the mercy seat that [is] over the testimony, where I will meet with thee.
7. And Aaron shall burn thereon sweet incense every morning: when he dresseth the lamps, he shall burn incense upon it.
8. And when Aaron lighteth the lamps at even, he shall burn incense upon it, a perpetual incense before the LORD throughout your generations. (KJV)

Sacred incense was burned day and night, representing prayers rising up, as a sweet fragrance to God. This is also described in the book of Psalm.

Psalm 141:2

Let my prayer be set forth before thee [as] incense; [and] the lifting up of my hands [as] the evening sacrifice. (KJV)

3. The Most Holy Place; The Holy of Holies

Only the high priest could enter the most holy place, and only once a year; to bring sacrifice to atone for the people's sins. In the most holy place, there was one most sacred item, *"the ark"*, called the ark of covenant or the ark of testimony. Within the ark were the following items:

1. Aaron's rod which budded, as a symbol against rebellion to God-given authority.

Numbers 17:8-10

8. And it came to pass, that on the morrow Moses went into the tabernacle of witness; and, behold, the rod of Aaron for the house of Levi was budded, and brought forth buds, and bloomed blossoms, and yielded almonds.

9. And Moses brought out all the rods from before the LORD unto all the children of Israel: and they looked, and took every man his rod.

10. And the LORD said unto Moses, Bring Aaron's rod again before the testimony, to be kept for a token against the rebels; and thou shalt quite take away their murmurings from me, that they die not. (KJV)

2. A pot of manna (an omer of manna) which represents supernatural provision and freedom from bondage.

Exodus 16:30-34

30. So the people rested on the seventh day.
31. And the house of Israel called the name thereof Manna: and it [was] like coriander seed, white; and the taste of it [was] like wafers [made] with honey.
32. And Moses said, this [is] the thing which the LORD commandeth, fill an omer of it to be kept for your generations; that they may see the bread wherewith I have fed you in the wilderness, when I brought you forth from the land of Egypt.
33. And Moses said unto Aaron, take a pot, and put an omer full of manna therein, and lay it up before the LORD, to be kept for your generations.
34. As the LORD commanded Moses, so Aaron laid it up before the Testimony, to be kept. (KJV)

3. The stone tablet with the Ten Commandments, also called *"the testimony"*, which represents the perfect Word, manifested in our lives.

> ***Exodus 24:12***
> *And the LORD said unto Moses, come up to me into the mount, and be there: and I will give thee tables of stone, and a law, and commandments which I have written; that thou mayest teach them. (KJV)*

4. The Ark of the Covenant. This was covered with a special lid or top called the "mercy seat", also known as the atonement seat or the atonement cover. It was made of pure gold with two Cherubim facing each other, towering over the mercy seat. God's Shekinah glory dwelt here. The tabernacle of Moses was the temporary place of worship that Moses built according to the specification of God while in the wilderness, and it was used until king Solomon built the temple. The most holy place was built in such a way that man, angels, cherubim and God can relate.

The Tabernacle Implications

We speak about the tabernacle in past tense because it only represents a picture of God's ultimate tabernacle; heaven, where God dwells.

Hebrews 9:11-13

11. But Christ came as High Priest of the good things to come, with the greater and more perfect tabernacle not made with hands, that is, not of this creation.

12. Not with the blood of goats and calves, but with His own blood He entered the Most Holy Place once for all, having obtained eternal redemption.

13. For if the blood of bulls and goats and the ashes of a heifer, sprinkling the unclean, sanctifies for the purifying of the flesh, (NKJV)

The attention to detail which the Lord displayed in constructing His tabernacle, shows how important His house is, and how we must prioritize it as His children. The outer court represents the flesh of man, the holy place represents man's soul, while the most holy place represents man's spirit.

The outer court which was lit by the natural sun, represents everything that is controlled by our physical senses. We can never relate with God in the flesh.

John 4:24

God is Spirit, and those who worship Him must worship in spirit and truth." (NKJV)

Therefore, studying and understanding all the items within the tabernacle and what they represent, helps us know where exactly we are in our relationship with God. Are we in the outer court, the holy place or the most holy place? Remember also that God's ultimate place of abode is inside every believer.

1 Corinthians 3:16

Do you not know that you are the temple of God and that the Spirit of God dwells in you? (NKJV)

If God dwells in heaven, and has made His home inside us, it means that every believer carries heaven on the inside. Hence, Jesus tore the veil to make a way for the hosts of heaven (angels, twenty-four elders and so on), to come inside man. This is indeed, a great mystery.

Prayer Point

Thank You Heavenly Father for revealing this great light to us, and for showing us exactly how it relates to us, as the temples in which You have chosen to dwell. Dear Lord, please help us apply this revelation to our lives as we grow in our walk with You. In Jesus' most holy Name we pray, Amen.

CHAPTER THREE

The Keepers of the Tabernacle

📖 The Levites.

God spoke to Moses in the wilderness of Sinai at the tent of meeting, on the first day of the second month, in the second year after they left Egypt.

God told him to number all the congregation of the people of Israel by their families, by clan, and by the house of their fathers, writing down the name of every male from twenty years and older, who was able to go to war. This he did with Aaron. He numbered them in the wilderness of Sinai; the children of Reuben, Simeon, Gad, Judah, Issachar and Zebulun. The children of Joseph namely; Ephraim and Manasseh, Benjamin, Dan, Asher and Naphtali, all totaling 603,550. The Levites were not counted by their ancestral family along with others. They belonged to God and were to take care of the tabernacle of testimony, including all the vessels, furnishings and all that belonged to the tabernacle.

Out of the family of the Levites was a particular family chosen by God as the family of priests; Aaron's family. Aaron was ordained as the high priest while his sons, Nadab the first born, Abihu, Eleazar and Ithamar, were anointed, consecrated and ordained to minister in the priest's office. Nadab the firstborn, and Abihu, died before the Lord when they offered strange fire (an unauthorized sacrifice), in the wilderness of Sinai and they had no sons. So only Eleazar and Ithamar served as priests during the life-time of their father Aaron.

The remaining Levites were presented to Aaron the high priest, to serve and assist him in the tabernacle. They became his assistants (servants and helpers), assigned wholly fulltime to work with him. Anyone that was not of the tribe of Levi who approached the tabernacle was put to death but the Levites encamped around the tabernacle so that the wrath of God will not fall on Israel.

The Descendants of Levi

Genesis 29:34

And she conceived again, and bare a son; and said, Now this time will my husband be joined unto me, because I have born him three sons: therefore was his name called Levi. (KJV)

Levi was the third son of Jacob born to him by Leah.

1 Chronicles 6:1-3

The sons of Levi; Gershon, Kohath, and Merari. And the sons of Kohath; Amram, Izhar, and Hebron, and Uzziel. And the children of Amram; Aaron, and Moses, and Miriam. The sons also of Aaron; Nadab, and Abihu, Eleazar, and Ithamar. (KJV)

Levi had three sons namely; Gershon, Kohath and Merari.

Gershon the Father of the Gershonites

The families of the Gershonites camped behind the tabernacle on the west side and this family was headed by Eliasaph the son of Lael. They were in charge of the external furnishing of the Tabernacle; the curtains of the courtyard that surrounded the tabernacle and the altar and the cords. They were numbered 7,500. They served under Ithamar the son of Aaron the high priest.

The Kohathites

They were responsible for the care of the sanctuary and the males were numbered 8,600. The head of the house of the Kohathites was Elzaphan, son of Uzziel; and their daily duty included the ark, the table, the lampstand, the altars and the utensils of the sanctuary used in worship. They handled the interiors. They took care of the most holy (sacred things). When Aaron and his sons had finished covering the holy furnishings, and all the holy articles, and the camp was ready to move, the Kohathites came in to do the carrying.

To protect them from death, God instructed Moses to make Aaron and his sons to always proceed before them into the sanctuary, and assign each person to his work, that is, who to carry what. Each person was given a specific duty or load to carry. Aaron lined up everyone to be sure the right person carried what they ought to carry. They were not to go in to look at the holy things in the holy and most holy place, not even a glance, or they would die. They were not allowed to put the ark on the cart, but were to bear it on their shoulders. They served under Eleazar the son of Aaron the high priest.

Numbers 4:15

And when Aaron and his sons have made an end of covering the sanctuary, and all the vessels of the sanctuary, as the camp is to set forward; after that, the sons of Kohath shall come to bear [it]: but they shall not touch [any] holy thing, lest they die. These [things are] the burden of the sons of Kohath in the tabernacle of the congregation. (KJV)

The Merarites

Chapter Three – The Keepers of the Tabernacle

They carried the frames, bars, pillars, sockets, bases, pegs and cords. And they were assigned by the name of the article which they were to carry on the match, and they were under the direction of Ithamar, son of Aaron the high priest.

Do we see the attention to detail which the Lord Almighty gives every act of service in His house? If we have not been this detailed about the things of God, this is the perfect moment to be smitten in our spirit, and repent.

In the next chapter, we will see how the sons of Korah rebelled against God, and learn some deeper lessons about our approach to serving God.

Prayer Point

Father in the Name of Jesus, we are forever grateful that You never leave us stranded. Please keep us forever humble and satisfied in any duty You assign to us in Your house. In Jesus' most precious Name we pray. Amen.

CHAPTER FOUR

The Rebellion of Korah

Numbers 16:1-24

1. Now Korah, the son of Izhar, the son of Kohath, the son of Levi, and Dathan and Abiram, the sons of Eliab, and On, the son of Peleth, sons of Reuben, took [men]:

2. And they rose up before Moses, with certain of the children of Israel, two hundred and fifty princes of the assembly, famous in the congregation, men of renown:

3. And they gathered themselves together against Moses and against Aaron, and said unto them, [Ye take] too much upon you, seeing all the congregation [are] holy, every one of them, and the LORD [is] among them:

wherefore then lift ye up yourselves above the congregation of the LORD?

4. And when Moses heard [it], he fell upon his face:

5. And he spake unto Korah and unto all his company, saying, Even to morrow the LORD will shew who [are] his, and [who is] holy; and will cause [him] to come near unto him: even [him] whom he hath chosen will he cause to come near unto him.

6. This do; Take you censers, Korah, and all his company;

7. And put fire therein, and put incense in them before the LORD tomorrow: and it shall be [that] the man whom the LORD doth choose, he [shall be] holy: [ye take] too much upon you, ye sons of Levi.

8. And Moses said unto Korah, Hear, I pray you, ye sons of Levi:

9. [Seemeth it but] a small thing unto you, that the God of Israel hath separated you from the congregation of Israel, to bring you near to himself to do the service of the tabernacle of the LORD, and to stand before the congregation to minister unto them?

10. And he hath brought thee near [to him], and all thy brethren the sons of Levi with thee: and seek ye the priesthood also?

11. For which cause [both] thou and all thy company [are] gathered together against the LORD: and what [is] Aaron, that ye murmur against him?

12. And Moses sent to call Dathan and Abiram, the sons of Eliab: which said, We will not come up:

13. [Is it] a small thing that thou hast brought us up out of a land that floweth with milk and honey, to kill us in the wilderness, except thou make thyself altogether a prince over us?

14. Moreover thou hast not brought us into a land that floweth with milk and honey, or given us inheritance of fields and vineyards: wilt thou put out the eyes of these men? we will not come up.

15. And Moses was very wroth, and said unto the LORD, Respect not thou their offering: I have not taken one ass from them, neither have I hurt one of them.

16. And Moses said unto Korah, Be thou and all thy company before the LORD, thou, and they, and Aaron, to morrow:

17. And take every man his censer, and put incense in them, and bring ye before the LORD every man his censer, two hundred and fifty censers; thou also, and Aaron, each [of you] his censer.
18. And they took every man his censer, and put fire in them, and laid incense thereon, and stood in the door of the tabernacle of the congregation with Moses and Aaron.
19. And Korah gathered all the congregation against them unto the door of the tabernacle of the congregation: and the glory of the LORD appeared unto all the congregation.
20. And the LORD spake unto Moses and unto Aaron, saying,
21. Separate yourselves from among this congregation, that I may consume them in a moment.
22. And they fell upon their faces, and said, O God, the God of the spirits of all flesh, shall one man sin, and wilt thou be wroth with all the congregation?
23. And the LORD spake unto Moses, saying,
24. Speak unto the congregation, saying, Get you up from about the tabernacle of Korah, Dathan, and Abiram. (KJV)

This is the third rebellion that Moses had to deal with. The first was when Aaron and Miriam opposed him for marrying an Ethiopian woman (Numbers 12:1-10). Mariam became leprous for speaking against Moses.

The second was when the spies went to the land of Canaan and returned with an evil report of the land. (Numbers 13:25-30; 14:1-6)

Moses begged and apologized on their behalf, but God did not let go. God came down heavily with His wrath. Even after the death of 250 people, the people still came back the following day accusing Moses of killing Korah and his men. The wrath of God came down again and another 14,700 people died.

Proverbs 13:3
He that keepeth his mouth keepeth his life: [but] he that openeth wide his lips shall have destruction.(KJV)

The Children of Korah.

Interestingly, just a few chapters later, during a God-ordained census, Scriptures reveal that the sons of Korah were spared from the judgment and punishment of God.

Numbers 26:9-11

9. And the sons of Eliab; Nemuel, and Dathan, and Abiram. This [is that] Dathan and Abiram, [which were] famous in the congregation, who strove against Moses and against Aaron in the company of Korah, when they strove against the LORD:

10. And the earth opened her mouth, and swallowed them up together with Korah, when that company died, what time the fire devoured two hundred and fifty men: and they became a sign.

*11. Notwithstanding **the children of Korah died not.***

(KJV)

The Bible does not explicitly state why the children of Korah were saved, but Bible scholars infer that either they were too young to join the rebellion against God, or they did not side with their father in his opposition.

It could also be that they were already grown up, and were not part of the household. They had probably made a decision to stand with the Lord, and not with their earthly father. It may also be that they came out at the last minute as Moses commanded the crowd to *'depart from them'.* Whatever be the case, Korah's children lived.

Perhaps the most interesting thing about the saved sons of Korah, is the way they were graciously used in the service of God in years to come. The prophet Samuel was a descendant of Korah.

1 Chronicles 6:31-38

31. These David put over the service of song in the house of the Lord after the ark of the covenant rested there [after being taken by the Philistines and later placed in the house of Abinadab, where it remained for nearly 100 years during the rest of Samuel's judgeship and Saul's entire reign and into David's reign].
32. They ministered before the tabernacle of the Tent of Meeting with singing until Solomon had built the Lord's house in Jerusalem, performing their service in due order.

33. These and their sons served of the **Kohathites:** Heman, the singer, the son of Joel, the son of **Samuel** [the great prophet and judge],

34. The son of Elkanah [III], the son of Jeroham, the son of Eliel, the son of Toah,

35. The son of Zuph, the son of Elkanah [II], the son of Mahath, the son of Amasai,

36. The son of Elkanah [I], the son of Joel, the son of Azariah, the son of Zephaniah,

37. The son of Tahath, the son of Assir, the son of Ebiasaph, **the son of Korah,**

38. The son of Izhar, the son of Kohath, the son of Levi, the son of Israel (Jacob). (AMP)

The Korahites were assigned the task of being custodians and door keepers for the tabernacle.

1 Chronicles 9:19-23

19. And Shallum the son of Kore, the son of Ebiasaph, the son of Korah, and his brethren, of the house of his father, the Korahites, [were] over the work of the service, keepers of the gates of the tabernacle: and their fathers, [being] over the host of the LORD, [were] keepers of the entry.

> 20. And Phinehas the son of Eleazar was the ruler over them in time past, [and] the LORD [was] with him.
> 21. [And] Zechariah the son of Meshelemiah [was] porter of the door of the tabernacle of the congregation.
> 22. All these [which were] chosen to be porters in the gates [were] two hundred and twelve. These were reckoned by their genealogy in their villages, whom David and Samuel the seer did ordain in their set office.
> 23. So they and their children [had] the oversight of the gates of the house of the LORD, [namely], the house of the tabernacle, by wards. (KJV)

Among King David's military men were a group of Korahites, commended for their expertise (1 Chronicles 12:1-6).

The Sons of Korah in The Psalms

Most touchingly, the sons of Korah were included amongst the writers of the psalms. They are credited with writing Psalms 42, 44, 45, 46, 47, 48, 49, 84, 85,

87, and 88. Among these psalms are psalms that express the longing, high appetite for God and His house, and total devotion and dedication to the things of God. Others provide images of deep humility and recognition of man as mere dust before a holy God. Sometimes you see glimpses of their forefathers dreadful past seep into some of these verses. They totally longed for the God their forefathers forsook.

Psalm 42:1-2

As the hart panteth after the water brooks, so panteth my soul after thee, O God. My soul thirsteth for God, for the living God: when shall I come and appear before God? (KJV)

Psalm 42:4

When I remember these [things], I pour out my soul in me: for I had gone with the multitude, I went with them to the house of God, with the voice of joy and praise, with a multitude that kept holyday. (KJV)

Psalm 46:1-4

1. God [is] our refuge and strength, a very present help in trouble.

2. Therefore will not we fear, though the earth be removed, and though the mountains be carried into the midst of the sea;
3. [Though] the waters thereof roar [and] be troubled, [though] the mountains shake with the swelling thereof. Selah.
4. [There is] a river, the streams whereof shall make glad the city of God, the holy [place] of the tabernacles of the most High. (KJV)

Psalm 46:5

God [is] in the midst of her; she shall not be moved: God shall help her, [and that] right early. (KJV)

Psalm 46:10

Be still, and know that I [am] God: I will be exalted among the heathen, I will be exalted in the earth. (KJV)

Psalm 49:20

Man [that is] in honour, and understandeth not, is like the beasts [that] perish. (KJV)

Psalm 84:1-2

How amiable [are] thy tabernacles, O LORD of hosts! My soul longeth, yea, even fainteth for the courts of the LORD: my heart and my flesh crieth out for the living God. (KJV)

Psalm 84:10

For a day in thy courts [is] better than a thousand. I had rather be a doorkeeper in the house of my God, than to dwell in the tents of wickedness. (KJV)

Psalm 87:1-3

*1. His foundation [is] in the holy mountains.
2. The LORD loveth the gates of Zion more than all the dwellings of Jacob.
3. Glorious things are spoken of thee, O city of God. Selah. (KJV)*

Psalm 87:5-7

*5. And of Zion it shall be said, This and that man was born in her: and the highest himself shall establish her.
6. The LORD shall count, when he writeth up the people, [that] this [man] was born there. Selah.*

> 7. As well the singers as the players on instruments [shall be there]: all my springs [are] in thee. (KJV)

The humble cry expressed throughout these psalms, rings clearly with an understanding of their ancestor's sin, which they never wanted to be part of.

The remnant of the sons of Korah even looked far into the future, and saw the salvation and redemption, through Jesus the Christ.

Psalm 49:7-9

> 7. None [of them] can by any means redeem his brother, nor give to God a ransom for him:
> 8. (For the redemption of their soul [is] precious, and it ceaseth for ever:)
> 9. That he should still live for ever, [and] not see corruption. (KJV)

Psalm 49:15

> But God will redeem my soul from the power of the grave: for he shall receive me. Selah. (KJV)

Lessons About the Sons of Korah

A few lessons about the sons of Korah, are beneficial to the body of Christ today.

* **Devotion:** They were devoted to God despite ancestral failures. These men were devoted to the Lord despite what they witnessed in their family lineage. We do not have to walk in the sins of our past, or that of our forefathers. They had the courage to stand with God no matter what their father chose.

* **Modesty:** No duty is too small in the house of God, all we need to do is obey. Never consider yourself too big to do seemingly small things, which God requires of you; just do it. They could have missed the miracle at Cana, if the servants had not obeyed the instruction of Jesus.

John 2:5
Jesus' mother then told the servants, "Do whatever he tells you." (GNT)

Anything that involves God can never be small, for it is a privilege and honor to be included in God's Kingdom. In this Kingdom, no task is of no significance, no matter the visibility and accolades, or the lack of them. Just like a big puzzle, all the pieces are needed. We scramble to look for even the tiny lost piece, otherwise the puzzle is incomplete.

So it is with the plan of God; everything fits together beautifully. We do not have to see the whole picture before we do our part. As gatekeepers, the sons of Korah understood the seriousness of what to let into their hearts, lives and worship before the Lord. Supporting David at the risk of their lives, they knew what mattered; standing with God and His anointed ones. God sees the big picture and a life of faith obeys Him even without seeing (Hebrews 11:1).

* A heart for God: They demonstrated an awe for God's holiness and power, as revealed in their service to the Lord in the temple, and their longing for God and His house. God extended mercy to the sons of Korah, and their hearts were true to Him.

* Qualified by God: Korah's descendants did not have to bear the sins of their prideful father, and that in itself was a blessing. It is so easy for arrogance and pride to creep into our minds and hearts, even while we work for the Lord. We must constantly guard against the prideful feeling that God needs us more than we need Him.

* **Humility:** They were humble before the Lord. They only needed to look back at their family ancestry, and remember how their forefather stood by his tent, and the ground that was beneath him split open and swallowed him. Korah's household and all the men who belonged to him, with their possessions, were also swallowed up, except these sons.

I will rather be at the center of God's will, doing the exact things that He has for me to do (no matter how small, invisible or insignificant in the eyes of men), than go off doing something else on my own, outside His will.

* **Satisfaction in God:** The sons of Korah were completely satisfied doing just what God set them apart to do. Unlike their forefathers, there was truly

no better place to be than in God's house, and in His presence.

Prayer Point

Father in the Name of Jesus, just like the sons of Korah, please cause Your Church to value You above all else, and let this reflect in our attitude towards Your Kingdom assignments. In Jesus' Mighty Name. Amen.

CHAPTER FIVE

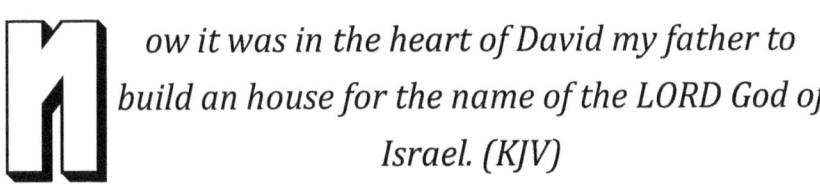

2 Chronicles 6:7

ow it was in the heart of David my father to build an house for the name of the LORD God of Israel. (KJV)

These were King Solomon's words as he was about to dedicate the temple in Jerusalem. He made reference to the motivation that led to the building of the temple; the desire of his father David.

2 Samuel 7:1-2

And it came to pass, when the king sat in his house, and the LORD had given him rest round about from all his

> enemies; That the king said unto Nathan the prophet, See now, I dwell in an house of cedar, but the ark of God dwelleth within curtains. (MSG)

Invariably, David said this in his heart, *"I still have a desire in my heart, for my desire was never fame, nor prosperity nor rest. Now that You have given me rest, my heart is still on You oh Lord".* And God was watching and listening to the contemplations of David's heart that will not rest until a house was built for his God, in his life time (2 Samuel 7:4-5; 7:8-18).

David dwelt in peace, free from war and lack, yet he had a desire for God to find a resting place. Even when God told David that He had seen his heart's desire, but he had shed too much blood to be qualified to build a house for Him, David was not offended. David was willing to get the raw materials and keep them for the person, who God will use to build His temple. He earnestly desired that the person would be someone that came from his loins. David's heart was knitted to his God.

Factors that determine the Presence of God
1. The Heart Condition:

The number one factor that controls the manifestation of the hand and the presence of God in a man's life, is the man's heart condition. The heart condition of a man according to Scriptures and in my experience, is the greatest determinant of the presence, power and grace of God. We have been taught that the secret to the manifestation of God's power and the glory, is praying and fasting. This is correct, only if the heart is right.

Every other thing in this Kingdom finds its place when your heart condition is right. No matter the spiritual activities you are involved in, if your desires and motives have not passed the screening and editing phase of God's X-ray, you may never host certain dimensions of God's presence and power.

Proverbs 16:2
People may be pure in their own eyes, but the LORD examines their motives. (NLT)

Herein lays the frustration of many believers who are actively engaged in spiritual activities, but never seem to carry the level of presence and glory of God that they desire. You must deal with the heart factor.

2. When all needs are met:

Secondly you cannot know if you truly love God when you have unmet needs; you know if you truly love God, when all your needs are met. There is something about the state of a man's heart when he has no more needs, his true character is revealed. I pray for an impartation of the desire of David in our hearts in the most holy Name of Jesus. Amen.

It must come upon your heart that you behold wealth, riches, self-actualization in your ministry and profession, and still come before God with a great desire. The desire for God in the beginning, when there were unmet needs, still blazing hot after all possible needs have been met. As simple as this is, it is mandatory if it is the God of heaven you want to walk with, and carry His presence, power, grace, and be entrusted with His influence over nations and territories, beyond praying, fasting and spiritual activities.

The heart of man is the greatest factor that invites God to tabernacle with man. The desire of David can inspire you and change your life today. Why would a king who has found rest round about, have such a burning desire? Do you know what it means to have rest round about? You have estates and houses all over the world, accolades to your name, obedient children who are doing so well that succession is in place. What do you need God for again?

David said, *"I have a desire, Prophet Nathan, help me tell God I will not rest till I find a place for Him in my life time"*. *"Lord I will not rest until everything you have given me, praises you"*. That was the heart cry of David. Do you know that every time God sees men who are ready to give all, to prove how much they love Him, they attract His attention immediately? Now you will understand this verse of scripture;

John 14:21-23

21. He that hath my commandments, and keepeth them, he it is that loveth me: and he that loveth me shall be loved of my Father, and I will love him, and will manifest myself to him.

> *22. Judas saith unto him, not Iscariot, Lord, how is it that thou wilt manifest thyself unto us, and not unto the world?*
> *23. Jesus answered and said unto him, If a man love me, he will keep my words: and my Father will love him, and we will come unto him, and make our abode with him. (KJV)*

You become a walking, living ark, carrying the presence of God everywhere you go. Then your life becomes a sign and a wonder, first to yourself, and then to everyone who cares to see. The secret behind the exploits of men, behind the seeming greatness you see, is the covenant that God finds hearts that live to glorify Him only, in life and in death. Just let men see God in you, and there is nothing God will not give to you.

Proverbs 23:26

> *My son, give me thine heart, and let thine eyes observe my ways. (KJV)*

What is God asking for 'you'? Not your offering or tithes, nor your singing, prophetic acumen or ministry. You can give God every other thing but if these things are devoid of your heart, it means you have not given Him anything. The train that carries every other thing to God, is your heart.

Mark 14:4

And there were some that had indignation within themselves, and said, Why was this waste of the ointment made? (KJV)

This Scripture implies that every time you see this desire, you will be tempted to think it's a waste of time; a waste of life. They called an expression of desire and hunger for Jesus, *a waste*. Remember the joy that was in David's heart when the ark was being restored, he was dancing and dancing, and Saul's daughter looked at him with disdain.

2 Samuel 6:16

As the Box was being brought into the city, Michal, Saul's daughter, looked out of the window and saw King David dancing and jumping around in the sacred dance, and she was disgusted with him. (GNT)

2 Samuel 6:20

When David returned home to bless his own family, Michal, the daughter of Saul, came out to meet him. She said in disgust, "How distinguished the king of Israel looked today, shamelessly exposing himself to the servant girls like any vulgar person might do!" (NLT)

2 Samuel 6:21-23

*21. David answered, "I was dancing to honor the LORD, who chose me instead of your father and his family to make me the leader of his people Israel.
22. And I will go on dancing to honor the LORD, and will disgrace myself even more. You may think I am nothing, but those women will think highly of me!"
23. Michal, Saul's daughter, never had any children. (GNT)*

God heard Michal and she died barren.

The real secret to God's presence is when you get to a point where you have the desire of David. This is the reason God made covenants with him. The sure mercies of David. Do you have a desire for his presence? God seeks union with man; He seeks to tabernacle with man.

John 14:23

Jesus answered and said to him, "If anyone loves Me, he will keep My word; and My Father will love him, and

We will come to him and make Our abode with him.
(NASB)

All through Scriptures, we see His intention not just to visit man, but to tabernacle with him. However, God is a God of systems and principles. In as much as He *is* love, He has exalted His Word, even above His Name. This means He is constrained by the principles of His Word. That is why as powerful as God is, He did not cast sin out of man, the way you cast out a demon but he had to go through the protocol that allowed for the remission of sin.

According to God's holy law, without the shedding of the blood, there cannot be remission of sin. Jesus had to submit Himself to the law, and pass through due process. It took thirty-three and a half years (the number of Jesus' years on earth), in the flesh, for man's sin to be dealt with, based on due process. God is a God of principles and He will not violate His principles. Please give Him your heart today, and make the desire for God and His house, your utmost priority in life.

Psalm 27:4

One [thing] have I desired of the LORD, that will I seek after; that I may dwell in the house of the LORD all the days of my life, to behold the beauty of the LORD, and to enquire in his temple. (KJV)

This was the desire of David. What is your desire and what is in your heart towards the Creator of your soul?

Prayer Point

Father in the Name of Jesus, we are indeed grateful for the example of David that You revealed to us in Your Word. Please cause our hearts to pant after You, that we might be called a people after Your heart. In Jesus' Name we pray, Amen.

CHAPTER SIX

The Manifest Presence of God

≣≣ *If the 23rd psalm be the most popular, the 103rd the most joyful, the 119th the most deeply experiential, the 51st the most plaintive, then the 84th is the sweetest of all".*
The noblest of the Song of Songs
C. H. Spurgeon

Psalm 84:1-2
How amiable [are] thy tabernacles, O LORD of hosts! My soul longeth, yea, even fainteth for the courts of the LORD: my heart and my flesh crieth out for the living God. (KJV)

It is possible for someone to mistake the presence of God for something very mundane, earthly, sensual or emotional. A lot of Christians believe that because they are crying with their eyes closed, they are in the presence of God.

If you are born again, you have the Holy Spirit. According to this verse below, you are in the Spirit.

Romans 8:9

But ye are not in the flesh, but in the Spirit, if so be that the Spirit of God dwell in you. Now if any man have not the Spirit of Christ, he is none of his. (KJV)

It is possible for someone to be born again and still tell lies, fornicate and commit all manner of atrocities. God is everywhere, but He does not manifest everywhere.

Psalm 139:7-12

7. Whither shall I go from thy spirit? or whither shall I flee from thy presence?

8. If I ascend up into heaven, thou [art] there: if I make my bed in hell, behold, thou [art there].

9. [If] I take the wings of the morning, [and] dwell in the uttermost parts of the sea;
10. Even there shall thy hand lead me, and thy right hand shall hold me.
11. If I say, Surely the darkness shall cover me; even the night shall be light about me.
12. Yea, the darkness hideth not from thee; but the night shineth as the day: the darkness and the light [are] both alike [to thee]. (KJV)

We are talking about the manifest, conscious presence of God. You are in the presence of God, when the influence of God's life and essence, rules and regulates you. Hence, you don't only have the Holy Spirit in your life, but the essence of the mind, will, and counsel of God controls and regulates your life.

If this is your experience, then you must recognize that you are in the presence of God. That is why we said earlier, that the presence of God is not only in crying or being emotional, that is just a measure of it. Sometimes you may cry, especially when you are overwhelmed, you might find yourself crying.

The presence of God is the establishment of the rulership of God upon a man's life. When a man is perpetually under the government of God, he walks from the realm of God's presence.

Revelation 21:3

And I heard a great voice out of heaven saying, Behold, the tabernacle of God [is] with men, and he will dwell with them, and they shall be his people, and God himself shall be with them, [and be] their God. (KJV)

The above Scripture describes people who live perpetually in and under the ambience and the control of God, and they are God's people. They are not just carriers of God's image, but they express the reality (present hour reality) of God. God is so real in their lives that you can touch God in them. God is their God, personally and intimately. He is their source and sustainer; He is their all. The totality of their reality is captured within the reality of God. This is what it means to be in the presence of God. And this is possible because the presence of God is majestic

1 Chronicles 16:27

Honor and majesty are [found] in His presence; strength and joy are [found] in His sanctuary. (AMP)

The majesty of God's presence brings His ruler-ship upon the man who is in His presence. When God shows up, he transmits His glory, splendor, majesty and honor upon the man. All these become the essence, nature and reality of that man. The presence of God confers the dominion of God upon a man. God rules and reigns supreme in his life.

Psalm 97:5

The hills melted like wax at the presence of the Lord, at the presence of the Lord of the whole earth. (AMP)

Because of the energy level and power of God's presence everything is compelled to conform to it. A man who lives by the flesh can never be said to be under the presence of God, no matter what he feels. God's presence is not defined by our feelings, but by our submission to the government and the ruler-ship of the reality that flows from His Kingdom realm.

Secondly, the presence of God is that which comes to reengineer every believer from within, so that we can take upon ourselves the very image of God.

You might be mentally conversant with most of the things that are written in this book, or even perhaps read it in Scriptures. However, have you experienced them as your reality? The indwelling presence of God is something a believer may have mentally, but not experientially.

Ephesians 3:19

[That you may really come] to know [practically, through experience for yourselves] the love of Christ, which far surpasses mere knowledge [without experience]; that you may be filled [through all your being] unto all the fullness of God [may have the richest measure of the divine Presence, and become a body wholly filled and flooded with God Himself]! (AMP)

Accessing the Presence of God via Brokenness

The divine being, YAHWEH, can only be pleased by the sacrifice of brokenness. The sons of Korah were broken men. They knew they were nothing without God.

Psalm 51:17

The sacrifices of God [are] a broken spirit: a broken and a contrite heart, O God, thou wilt not despise. (KJV)

Have you ever asked what is most important in the realm of the immortals? Because among mortal beings, healing the sick and raising the dead are classified as exploits. So, what do you do in a corridor where sickness, death, pain and sorrow do not exist? What do you do in the corridor of immortality, where raising the dead and healing the sick are not exploits? What is considered an exploit for the immortals? It is the ability to conform to the will of the Monarch that rules that realm, through brokenness. Mighty men of God's Kingdom realm, are broken men.

Psalm 34:18

> *The Lord is close to those who are of a **broken heart** and saves such as are crushed with sorrow for sin and are humbly and thoroughly penitent. (AMP)*

Brokenness in the eyes of God means to be broken, crushed, and torn in spirit over sin. In the books of 2 Samuel 12 and Psalms 51, we see the true meaning and beauty of brokenness. The Lord desires spiritual brokenness, the kind of brokenness He can use. He searches for godly sorrow that leads to repentance. And out of that desperation, out of the grief and hurt of a fractured heart over sin, God longs to produce humility in us. Humility is a virtue that allows us to recognize as David did, the person of God, and who we are in comparison to Him. Brokenness brings us back into fellowship with God.

Broken people are teachable, no matter their age, gender, educational qualification or race. They understand that being teachable means a ready willingness to admit when they are wrong, and do that freely, resting in God's unconditional acceptance of them.

Broken people are forgivers. They know that they have been fully forgiven of all their sins and shortcomings, past, present and future, and they know that true freedom comes when they forgive others.

Broken people are not control freaks. They understand that control is an illusion that insecure people cling to.

Broken people know that they cannot do anything of real eternal value in their own strength. They are like our Master Jesus Christ.

John 5:30

I am able to do nothing from Myself [independently, of My own accord--but only as I am taught by God and as I get His orders]. Even as I hear, I judge [I decide as I am bidden to decide. As the voice comes to Me, so I give a decision], and My judgment is right (just, righteous), because I do not seek or consult My own will [I have no desire to do what is pleasing to Myself, My own aim, My own purpose] but only the will and pleasure of the Father Who sent Me. (AMP)

They do not make arrogant statements like, *"I need to work on that weakness in me"*, because they understand that life in Christ is never about them trying to fix themselves or others. They are fully aware that it is only as they rest in Christ, as Christ rested in the Father, allowing Him to do His work in them, will their lives have lasting, life-giving impact.

Philippians 2:13

[Not in your own strength] for it is God Who is all the while effectually at work in you [energizing and creating in you the power and desire], both to will and to work for His good pleasure and satisfaction and delight. (AMP)

They rest in who they are in Christ. They do not have to know everything in a day and age that is obsessed with knowledge. An age that is still drunk from the juice of the tree of knowledge eaten by Adam and Eve (Genesis 3:6). Broken people rely on the fact that they don't need to know everything. They rest in God their Father, trusting that He always knows. They live in the assurance that it is okay to cry out and admit. *"We do not know what to do, but our eyes are on You oh Lord."*

2 Chronicles 20:12

O our God, wilt thou not judge them? for we have no might against this great company that cometh against us; neither know we what to do: but our eyes [are] upon thee. (KJV)

Broken people are free to love and accept people. With this lifestyle of love and acceptance, they draw other people to the only One Who is love.

1 John 4:8

He that loveth not knoweth not God; for God is love. (KJV)

They have laid down their rights before of God and He is Lord in all. They understand that they do not have any right whether to family, friends, houses, cars, and so on, because they have laid down their rights and lives in the reality that God is the giver of life, and all good things comes from him.

James 1:17

Every good gift and every perfect (free, large, full) gift is from above; it comes down from the Father of all [that gives] light, in [the shining of] Whom there can be no variation [rising or setting] or shadow cast by His turning [as in an eclipse]. (AMP)

Broken people are Kingdom oriented. They understand that they are first and foremost, citizens of God's Kingdom which is breaking forth on planet earth. They know that what is most important is getting to know God more, and getting to know who they are in Him; then all other things shall be added as God pleases.

Matthew 6:33

But seek ye first the kingdom of God, and his righteousness; and all these things shall be added unto you. (KJV)

They seek the truth always, knowing that Jesus is Truth. They have seen and testified to Jesus being the Truth that sets people free.

John 8:32

And ye shall know the truth, and the truth shall make you free. (KJV)

Broken people understand that true humility means agreeing with God, nothing more, nothing less. They understand that pride says, *"I am more than God and*

His Word". While humility says, *"I am less".* They realize that they cannot fix the wounds in their own souls. Therefore, they cry out to God to reveal the wounds and idols, and for Him to heal the wounds, bring down every idol in their lives, and set them free to live lives of abundance.

A broken man is a man that has come under the government and governance of God. The Holy Spirit has become the regulator of his life.

The Holy Spirit is allowed to operate unchecked, having access to operate and express Himself within, thereby bringing about a daily transformation. This is not a life of religion, rules and regulations, but a God-filled life. This transformed life confers on him, the power to enact the dominion mandate, which is the ability to bring creation under the government of God. It is only the broken that have access to the presence of God.

Prayer Point

Father in the Name of Jesus, please endue us with the spirit of brokenness, that we may never miss out on Your manifest presence in our daily lives. In Jesus Name, Amen.

CHAPTER SEVEN

The Civilization of Light in His Presence

> *In His presence is the civilization of light;*
> *In light there is no confusion".*

If Satan wants to steal from you through spiritual means, he throws you into confusion. Anything you do or any action or reaction you make under the influence of this confusion, will be wrong. The only strategic thing you can do in times of confusion, is to go back to God. Satan lurks around, seeking to make us walk in shadows, uncertainty, and within the corridors of confusion.

The Bible reveals various contexts, in which we can experience God and one of them is experiencing Him as Light. The Bible says that God is Light, and in Him, there is no darkness at all (1 John 1:5).

Ephesians 5:13

But all things that are exposed are made manifest by the light, for whatever makes manifest is light. (NKJV)

Furthermore, the Bible further reveals that everything is made manifest by light. It means therefore, that if you are confused, you have not met the Light. If you need to take a decision, and there is no clarity, you are still in darkness. You have not met Light because in the experience of God as Light, He makes all things manifest.

It is a terrible thing to grope in darkness without the light of God. If you move under the cover of darkness, you will come back home with Leah, instead of Rachel. Jacob married Leah, had intimacy with her in the dark and woke up with regrets when light came on (Genesis 29).

May you not make destiny decisions under the cover of darkness in Jesus' Name, Amen.

Some people may have felt they had light before choosing who to marry. Others felt they had light before they chose their job. But remember that the devil is going to have a harvest on whatever breakthrough you are anticipating, if the decisions that led to the foundation of that journey, were made in darkness.

Psalm 36:9

For with thee [is] the fountain of life: in thy light shall we see light. (KJV)

Psalm 36:9

For you are the fountain of life, the light by which we see. (NLT)

Confusion is a proof that you have not found light, and only in God's presence can you encounter light. You will live a contrary life, not intended by God for you, without light, and you will have a contrary destiny without light. The things seen by the power of the Holy Ghost are called 'true' in Scriptures. Therefore, if the only sight you have is that of your natural eyes, the Bible calls you blind.

1 Corinthians 2:14

But the natural, nonspiritual man does not accept or welcome or admit into his heart the gifts and teachings and revelations of the Spirit of God, for they are folly (meaningless nonsense) to him; and he is incapable of knowing them [of progressively recognizing, understanding, and becoming better acquainted with them] because they are spiritually discerned and estimated and appreciated. (AMP)

A careful study of Scriptures reveals that any time God wanted to help anyone in the Bible, God gave the person light. Joseph is a very good example;

Matthew 2:13

Now after they had gone, behold, an angel of the Lord appeared to Joseph in a dream and said, Get up! [Tenderly] take unto you the young Child and His mother and flee to Egypt; and remain there till I tell you [otherwise], for Herod intends to search for the Child in order to destroy Him. (AMP)

Matthew 2:19-20

But when Herod died, behold, an angel of the Lord appeared in a dream to Joseph in Egypt And said, Rise, [tenderly] take unto you the Child and His mother and go to the land of Israel, for those who sought the Child's life are dead. (AMP)

The light of God took him outside his geographical location for preservation, and the same light came again to give him insight as to when to return. God arranged for them to return because the fulfillment of the child's destiny, was within that specific geographical location.

Sadly, for many Christians, it is when Herod (the one who has been looking to kill us), gives us a scar, that we decide to obey the Light. If you do not have light, you will make yourself king in a place where God has left. Only when God sheds His light, do we begin to see our situation. If God doesn't shed light, we are without reference and that is a bad place to be.

John 8:12

Then spake Jesus again unto them, saying, I am the light of the world: he that followeth me shall not walk in darkness, but shall have the light of life. (KJV)

Whoever follows Jesus in truth and in deed, shall have access to the light which His life within gives. This

Scripture establishes the possibility of experiencing God as Light. There is an experience of God as Deliverer, Savior, Healer, Protector and Provider. But there is more. There are layers upon layers of experience in God, and experiencing Him as Light, beyond merely reading it in Scripture, is one of them.

When you get to know light experientially, you will detest walking in darkness. Anytime there is confusion, you will stop, and go for light because you know that any move made in darkness will lead to defeat, regret, waste of time and resources, and God forbids, loss of life.

The Standard of God Revealed in Light

The economy of light brings us to a point where we see, know and understand the standards of God. God has standards, and light affords every believer, the privilege of conforming to His standards. We cannot judge ourselves correctly, until we are placed under the light of God. This was prophet Isaiah's testimony:

Isaiah 6:1-5

1. In the year that king Uzziah died I saw also the Lord sitting upon a throne, high and lifted up, and his train filled the temple.
2. Above it stood the seraphims: each one had six wings; with twain he covered his face, and with twain he covered his feet, and with twain he did fly.
3. And one cried unto another, and said, Holy, holy, holy, [is] the LORD of hosts: the whole earth [is] full of his glory.
4. And the posts of the door moved at the voice of him that cried, and the house was filled with smoke.
5. Then said I, Woe [is] me! for I am undone; because I [am] a man of unclean lips, and I dwell in the midst of a people of unclean lips: for mine eyes have seen the King, the LORD of hosts. (KJV)

Having beheld the standard of God's glory and holiness, the great prophet Isaiah discovered that he was a man of unclean lips, though he was a major and national prophet. He was not aware of this until he came under the light of God, and the state of his heart was exposed in comparison to the standard of God.

In God's presence, His light exposes everything that needs to be dealt with, so that we can be more like Him. A man that is still comfortable in sin, has not experienced the presence of God. He may know it mentally or cerebrally, but he does not know it experientially. For he is not fully aware that his body is the temple of God, the very sanctuary of the Holy Ghost.

1 Corinthians 6:19

Or didn't you realize that your body is a sacred place, the place of the Holy Spirit? Don't you see that you can't live however you please, squandering what God paid such a high price for? The physical part of you is not some piece of property belonging to the spiritual part of you. (MSG)

The secret to accessing everything that is in God, is the indwelling presence of God. The indwelling presence of God can only be experienced by the spirit, not by the power of the flesh. Unfortunately, many Christians have formed the habit of confessing Scriptures and even praying, not by the energy of the Spirit but by the energy of the flesh. That is why the indwelling presence of God is elusive.

> **Galatians 3:3**
> *Are you so foolish and so senseless and so silly? Having begun [your new life spiritually] with the [Holy] Spirit, are you now reaching perfection [by dependence] on the flesh? (AMP)*

God is not man; He cannot be mocked. You cannot tap into spiritual energy by the flesh. Trying to do something that looks like faith in the flesh, does not convey the power of God. The grace to carry on our Christian walk only by the Spirit of God, is released afresh upon us in Jesus' mighty Name. Amen.

Journey from Flesh to Spirit

One of the first things God does as He takes us on an adventure into His presence, is to give us a revelation of His presence. Knowing his presence by revelation is different from knowing it mentally. This journey starts when we begin to pray or do anything that has to do with our spirits directly, such as meditation or worship.

For instance, we can begin a worship song or start a prayer from the flesh. There is nothing wrong with starting in the flesh because the resource base that God transmits from, within in our hearts is *"dunamis"*.

An English word derived from *"dunamis"* is *"dynamo"*. A dynamo is a device used to convert mechanical energy into electrical energy. Mechanical energy represents the flesh, while electrical energy represents the spirit. Hence, the *"dunamis"* within our hearts is used by God to move us from the realm of the flesh, to that of the spirit.

Hence, there is nothing wrong with starting your prayer, worship, or speaking in tongues from the flesh. However, you need to keep speaking in tongues until you are quickened by God's Spirit within. You cannot enter into God except God allows you. You cannot find the face of God unless you are quickened by His Spirit.

Psalm 80:18
So will not we go back from thee: quicken us, and we will call upon thy name. (KJV)

The spirit world is a vast expanse that requires the guidance of the Holy Spirit to operate in, lest we get lost. Our adventure with God therefore begins when the Spirit of God quickens our spirits. This quickening enlivens us, and brings us to a point where our senses begin to pick frequencies of the Spirit as they open up.

Prayer is not effective until our spirits are quickened. This quickening power impacts us with a sharp consciousness of the realm that we are attempting to trade in. Hence, we begin to mount up with wings like an eagle. The strength that drives us is no longer the strength with which we started praying, but that of God's Holy Spirit.

There is no need to exert too much energy, by shouting loudly in the place of prayer, when our spirits have not yet been quickened. That would be praying in the flesh. It drains the body, and quickens the aging process. God needs our mortal bodies to be strong, living long enough to do maximum damage to the kingdom of darkness.

Stop trying to seek God using carnal energy. When it is obvious that you have been quickened, you can then use the quickening energy to drive the machine. At this point, you are running by spirit power and the spirit realm has its own consciousness that will help facilitate your adventure within her borders. You are not in the flesh anymore, therefore you don't get to be in control of what you do in that realm, the Holy Spirit does.

At the point of being quickened, the Name of Jesus, the Blood of Jesus and the voice of God become more real to you. Mundane things are not found in the spirit realm. When you are quickened, even your tongues are more precise and distinct because a new level of consciousness has been opened up.

Profiting from the Spirit Realm

Many of us believers have been exposed to many valuable spiritual things that we did not get value from, because we have not been trained on how to profit from the presence of God. It is crucial to know how to profit from it, and how to practice His presence.

The spirit realm sustains its own inherent intelligence. So, thank God for your prayer points and all of that, but this realm is beyond your prayer points. Thank God for the tongues you speak and the ones you remember, but when you get to this realm, you won't remember the ones you are speaking, because it is not you that is talking, but God. Thank God for the things you know, but beyond your knowledge, it borders on the things you don't know, because the realm functions by revelation.

One very beautiful thing about the realm of God's Spirit is that it exposes areas of weakness that have hindered our spiritual growth and exploits. Once that weakness is revealed, for example bitterness or unforgiveness, it must be abandoned on the altar of sacrifice.

Romans 12:1
I APPEAL to you therefore, brethren, and beg of you in view of [all] the mercies of God, to make a decisive dedication of your bodies [presenting all your members and faculties] as a living sacrifice, holy (devoted, consecrated) and well pleasing to God, which is your

> *reasonable (rational, intelligent) service and spiritual worship. (AMP)*

The higher we rise in the realm of the spirit, the more God reveals negative attitudes and habits that must be dropped. However, many Christians have not risen higher in the realm of the spirit, because they have refused to let go of some of the things revealed by God.

Refusal to let go, is an indication of the fact that there is a part of you that is alive, apart from God. That part has been detected in the spirit realm, and is the doorway for the devil's exploitation of your life and destiny. Every time you gain a consciousness of God's emphasis on an area of your life, it is an act of great love to ensure that there's nothing around your life that the devil can exploit.

As terrible as the devil is, you do not have to be afraid of him. For you to live above the darkness of this world, you must dwell in the secret place of the Most High God, not just visit. God's intention is for us to dwell in the secret place; the Holy of holies.

Prayer Point

Father in the Name of Jesus, please help us never to take for granted, the importance of Your revelation light, as we grow in our relationship with You. In Jesus' Name, Amen.

CHAPTER EIGHT

Dwelling in His Light

Psalm 91:1-2

e that dwelleth in the secret place of the most High shall abide under the shadow of the Almighty. I will say of the LORD, [He is] my refuge and my fortress: my God; in him will I trust. (KJV)

Many believers come into the presence of God looking for healing. Meanwhile, what we should look for in that place is the emphasis of Jesus. What is Jesus saying? What has Jesus seen? What is Jesus probing in your life? The presence of God is a full habitat that has countless levels and realities. If we want to make progress with God, we must be sure to itemize the things that are probed in us by His Spirit. Our pens and paper should capture everything. These must become our prayer projects, because that have denied us access to the next higher levels in all facets of life.

The testimony about Samuel began from his attitude of honor, dignity and integrity, before that of his prophetic ministry.

1 Samuel 3:18-19

And Samuel told him every whit, and hid nothing from him. And he said, It [is] the LORD: let him do what seemeth him good. And Samuel grew, and the LORD was with him, and did let none of his words fall to the ground. (KJV)

1 Samuel 7:13-15

13. So the Philistines were subdued, and they came no more into the coast of Israel: and the hand of the LORD was against the Philistines all the days of Samuel.
14. And the cities which the Philistines had taken from Israel were restored to Israel, from Ekron even unto Gath; and the coasts thereof did Israel deliver out of the hands of the Philistines. And there was peace between Israel and the Amorites.

> *15. And Samuel judged Israel all the days of his life. (KJV)*

The place of intimacy and honor that God bequeathed to Samuel, gave him his superior identity among men. A lot of times, we are not released into the next higher levels in life because the issues that are probed by God, are not dealt with. When God deals with a thing, He usually leaves a scar, so that we always remember His loving dealings. So that like David, we are reminded of where He brought us from.

> **2 Samuel 7:8**
> *Now therefore so shalt thou say unto my servant David, Thus saith the LORD of hosts, I took thee from the sheepcote, from following the sheep, to be ruler over my people, over Israel: (KJV)*

"David, remember the sheepcote just in case pride is trying to set in". God in His love, gives us something that links us with a memory that brings us back in check. This is necessary because sometimes, when men are helped by God, they become too strong for God. We must have a system in place that reminds us that we are who we are, only by the grace of God.

Ephesians 2:8-9

For by grace you have been saved through faith, and that not of yourselves; it is the gift of God, not of works, lest anyone should boast. (NKJV)

Many have used the resources made available by God to run their own personal agenda. The level of negative feedback and stench that is coming from the body of Christ is scary. Hence, we all as a Church, need to know the presence of God afresh.

Most times, the item for probing does not look obvious, it could be friends or certain relationships which we have to let go. Do you know that you can be a good man and still suffer? Abraham was good by taking Lot with him but that was not God's instruction. As soon as Lot separated from Abraham, the Lord began speaking to Abraham again. It was as if God was waiting for Abraham to let go of Lot, before speaking.

Genesis 13:14-15

After Lot separated from him, GOD said to Abram, "Open your eyes, look around. Look north, south, east, and west. Everything you see, the whole land spread out before you, I will give to you and your children forever. (MSG)

Every new season in your life will demand something. Most of these things you will not find in Bible studies or Sunday school classes, until you are quickened to journey into the presence of God. I am writing this because God is calling upon His children, to give them the blue print and templates for an adventurous walk with Him.

Beloved, there is something God wants to tell you now that will become the essence of your life, and what He is expecting from your life this season. There are many things that are hidden in the government of His presence, which your eyes will never see outside His presence.

Proverbs 25:2
It is the glory of God to conceal a thing, but the glory of kings is to search out a thing. (AMP)

Many people that have been sent to destroy you, will discover how impotent they are, when you understand these mysteries. Your life will not end the negative way your forefathers' ended in Jesus' Name.

The people that God will use are not many so he will preserve the few that he has now.

Matthew 9:37

He said to his disciples, "The harvest is great, but the workers are few. (NLT)

They are not many, so I recommend that you take some time to go on this adventure because God has something to say. In His presence, your prayer points, your emphasis, the way you study your Bible, all of these will change. This is because you will begin to see something beyond what you are used to. A new season will change your life forever. God is eternal but He administers His purposes on the face of the earth in seasons, and times. This works in favor of every child of God that is in alignment with Him.

Please, put down this book now and pray:

Father in the Name of Jesus Christ, give me the strength to seek you deliberately and intentionally, until I find You. In Jesus Holy Name, Amen.

Heeding God's Call

God is calling you, and He is calling you now. Have you noticed a disorder in your environment or family? God might be saying that there is something that needs to shift. Stay long enough until He shows it to you. Something was preventing Abraham's destiny from manifesting; it was the presence of his nephew Lot. As long as he had Lot around him, well, God blessed Abraham as much as He could, but He could not implement His ultimate plan, in and through Abraham's life.

May God scatter any relationship that is hindering your destiny from blossoming, in Jesus' Mighty Name, Amen. The day for which we were saved and called in Jesus, just started now! All we have ever done, forms the foundation that has put us in gear, so that we survived up until this time. The reason for your calling is now! The time has come. He is calling you to intimacy, and God will take you beyond your wildest imagination.

Father in the Name of Jesus, we embrace the grace to tarry in Your presence, until our ears are quickened to hear, and our hearts begin to understand what is at stake.

The light of God also brings us into fellowship with the counsel of God, for it takes the wisdom of God for us to rule in life. Outside God's divine wisdom, our lives will be plagued with confusion, and we will journey far away from the path that is destined for us. The only way a man can journey accurately in destiny, is when he has access to light. This is what Daniel operated with:

Daniel 5:11-13

11. There is a man in thy kingdom, in whom [is] the spirit of the holy gods; and in the days of thy father light and understanding and wisdom, like the wisdom of the gods, was found in him; whom the king Nebuchadnezzar thy father, the king, [I say], thy father, made master of the magicians, astrologers, Chaldeans, [and] soothsayers;

12. Forasmuch as an excellent spirit, and knowledge, and understanding, interpreting of dreams, and shewing of hard sentences, and dissolving of doubts, were found in the same Daniel, whom the king named

Belteshazzar: now let Daniel be called, and he will shew the interpretation.
13. Then was Daniel brought in before the king. [And] the king spake and said unto Daniel, [Art] thou that Daniel, which [art] of the children of the captivity of Judah, whom the king my father brought out of Jewry? (KJV).

We are bound to struggle with the systems of this world, and with forces of darkness, until we learn how to navigate by the light of His presence. The light of God paves a pathway for an excellent life; a life of prevailing dominion (Genesis 1:28). Unfortunately, many Christians leave their lives to chance and luck. To them, Christianity is a lifestyle rules and regulations that do not work.

The life of a Christian should be born out of our intimacy with God. The more we know about God, the more we want to know. That's how it works. Our desire for His presence is always on the increase because every time we appear before Him, He gives us a part of Him that makes us long for more. This is the unending joy of dwelling in His light.

Prayer Point

Father in the Name of Jesus, please help us as a Church to constantly desire the dwelling place of Your light. In Jesus Name, Amen.

CHAPTER NINE

The Economy of Sound in His Presence

"THE VOICE OF GOD"

Our journey in the spirit is likened unto the kind of transitions that Abraham had to navigate, in search of his inheritance.

Genesis 12:1

Now the LORD had said to Abram: "Get out of your country, From your family And from your father's house, To a land that I will show you. (NKJV)

Notice in the above Scripture that the details of where Abraham was meant to go, was withheld. This is so that there could be fellowship between God and Abraham. Thus, every dream and every vision he had, was significant to his navigation. Every word that came from God, formed another section of the map for his navigation. Abraham's success was tied to his intimacy with God. It was therefore impossible for him to have a quarrel with God.

Genesis 23:3-4 (Paraphrase)

And Abraham stood up ... and said to the sons of Heth, I am a stranger and a sojourner with you; ... (AMP)

He was in a strange land not knowing his left from his right. His life and survival depended absolutely on hearing God. The voice of God communicates spiritual possibilities. Our lives will be dry, and void of interventions and spiritual resources, unless we hear from the realm of God. Only in His presence, can we triumph over all that are assigned by the devil and the world to pull us down.

For there is a way that seem right in the eyes of men but it only leads to destruction, ruin and decay

(Proverbs 14:12). Only in God's presence do we encounter destiny. There has never been a man that made any great impact in the Kingdom, without the statement, *'God said - - - , and God said'*. These men had access to the voice of God; to the sound of heaven. These came as ideas, inspirations that communicated supernatural, spiritual and physical possibilities.

"And they heard the voice of the LORD God walking in the garden in the cool of the day" (Genesis 3:8). This was how Adam dominated the Garden of Eden before the fall.

Revelation 1:9-11

9. I John, who also am your brother, and companion in tribulation, and in the kingdom and patience of Jesus Christ, was in the isle that is called Patmos, for the word of God, and for the testimony of Jesus Christ.

10. I was in the Spirit on the Lord's day, and heard behind me a great voice, as of a trumpet,

11. Saying, I am Alpha and Omega, the first and the last: and, What thou seest, write in a book, and send [it] unto the seven churches which are in Asia; unto Ephesus, and unto Smyrna, and unto Pergamos, and unto Thyatira, and unto Sardis, and unto Philadelphia, and unto Laodicea. (KJV)

Because of the voice of God, John did not function as a creature of time, but of eternity. You can never win in life and destiny until you have access to the sounds of heaven. If only we know how dependent we are supposed to be on our God, we will cherish every single moment in His presence. It is His presence that makes all the difference in a man's life.

There are several moments when heaven wants to orchestrate an intervention. In such a situation, if the participation of man is required, heaven quickens a *'summon'*. A summon is an invitation to come up to the realm of God. Do we remember the prescription that was given to Noah to build the ark? Exact specifications were given to him (Genesis 6:14-22). It means that God dictated to Noah, these dimensions. Noah's creativity was not required.

That is how God's call upon our lives is represented, and that is how the things of God are. They come custom made, and we are expected to yield, not to be re-creative about them. When God speaks, He is not asking for our opinion, but our simple obedience. Our call is not a call to creativity or strategy, but a call to yieldedness. As God's worthy vessels, we are expected to download unto the earth, something that already exists before God in heaven.

Matthew 6:10

Your kingdom come, Your will be done on earth as it is in heaven. (AMP)

Our lives, ministries and destinies were already measured, before we were given grace to execute them. Paul knew this when he said he was pressing on towards the mark of his life and ministry, to a mark of impact, coverage and influence, that his ministry should have, which is already known in heaven.

Philippians 3:14

I press toward the mark for the prize of the high calling of God in Christ Jesus. (KJV)

It was his yieldedness, tenacity and faithfulness on earth, to the sounds of heaven that produced the exploits he accomplished in his lifetime. Whenever we entertain an error, we miss the mark. Hence, the outcome will no longer be consistent with the standard expected. And there are many reasons that men and women become susceptible to error. One of them is ignorance. This we saw in the life of Solomon. His ultimate outcome was not God's expectation.

1 Kings 11:4

For it came to pass, when Solomon was old, [that] his wives turned away his heart after other gods: and his heart was not perfect with the LORD his God, as [was] the heart of David his father. (KJV)

Meanwhile, his father David, served his generation according to the will of God, the voice of God, and the instructions of God, and slept with his fathers.

Acts 13:36

For David, after he had served his own generation by the will of God, fell on sleep, and was laid unto his fathers, and saw corruption: (KJV)

The Bible is loaded with statements like; "and David enquired of the Lord"; "therefore David enquired of the Lord"; "then David enquired yet again of the Lord".

1 Samuel 23:2-4

2. Therefore David enquired of the LORD, saying, Shall I go and smite these Philistines? And the LORD said unto David, Go, and smite the Philistines, and save Keilah.

3. And David's men said unto him, Behold, we be afraid here in Judah: how much more then if we come to Keilah against the armies of the Philistines?
4. Then David enquired of the LORD yet again. And the LORD answered him and said, Arise, go down to Keilah; for I will deliver the Philistines into thine hand. (KJV)

2 Samuel 21:1

Then there was a famine in the days of David three years, year after year; and David enquired of the LORD. And the LORD answered, [It is] for Saul, and for [his] bloody house, because he slew the Gibeonites. (KJV)

1 Chronicles 14:10

And David enquired of God, saying, Shall I go up against the Philistines? and wilt thou deliver them into mine hand? And the LORD said unto him, Go up; for I will deliver them into thine hand. (KJV)

1 Chronicles 14:14

Therefore David enquired again of God; and God said unto him, Go not up after them; turn away from them, and come upon them over against the mulberry trees. (KJV)

That means David was a true representation of what God had in mind, before he died. We saw in the life of David, a living epistle; something that was living in heaven, that manifested through the yieldedness of a man, to the sounds of heaven. In his life, we saw the compatibility between worship and warfare. He was the chief worshipper as well as a master warrior.

All of that was unveiled through the testament and story of David's life. If you execute the will of God for your life accurately, it will be a clear story because your life in the spirit is a story that God is telling from heaven. Like the case of Balaam and Barak in Numbers 22.

Numbers 22:9-12

9. Then God came to Balaam. He asked, "So who are these men here with you?"

10. Balaam answered, "Balak son of Zippor, king of Moab, sent them with a message:

11. "Look, the people that came up out of Egypt are all over the place! Come and curse them for me. Maybe then I'll be able to attack and drive them out of the country."'

> 12. God said to Balaam, "Don't go with them. And don't curse the others--they are a blessed people." (MSG)

When Balaam went to God, God forbade him from making the trip. So, he knew God's position on the matter. When a man walks in error, it is not necessarily because of ignorance only; outright rebellion can be another factor. Carelessness and so many other factors can lead to error.

When this error becomes visible at the end of a man's pilgrimage, it becomes obvious to all, that the place where the man ended his assignment, is not where God intended. It is only the voice of God, and yielding to it that can terminate errors in the life of a man. In God's presence is the economy of His voice.

Prayer Point

Father in the Name of Jesus, please help us never to miss Your voice, as You beckon on us with sweet sounds of Your love. In Jesus' Name Amen.

CHAPTER TEN

Christ Revealed in His Presence

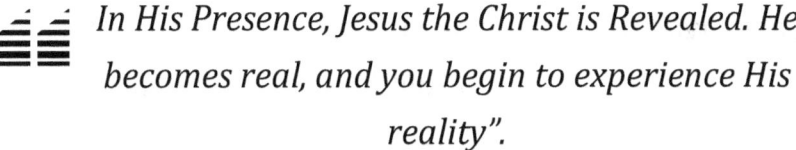

In His Presence, Jesus the Christ is Revealed. He becomes real, and you begin to experience His reality".

Luke 24:44
And he said unto them, These [are] the words which I spake unto you, while I was yet with you, that all things must be fulfilled, which were written in the law of Moses, and [in] the prophets, and [in] the psalms, concerning me. (KJV)

In the verse above, Jesus said that the law of Moses, the prophets, and the psalms (this was the Bible read in the earthly days of Jesus; the Old Testament), is all about Him. The Bible is not about the teaching of a subject, but is a Book that is put together to reveal a Person. Moses told the children of Israel that the Lord will raise a prophet like himself; that is a prophecy about Jesus.

Deuteronomy 18:15

The LORD thy God will raise up unto thee a Prophet from the midst of thee, of thy brethren, like unto me; unto him ye shall hearken;(KJV)

Moses was the pastor of the Church in the wilderness, and the situation of the wilderness was a situation of lack. There was neither water nor food in the wilderness. They did not have an army that could protect them from battle in the wilderness. All they had was a prophet called Moses. If they wanted water, they went to Moses, and Moses had a way of communicating their request to God, and hearing God's response.

Their civilization and survival in the wilderness was because they had God's man, Moses. And the same

Moses prophesied that a prophet like himself, whom they were going to depend on absolutely, will be raised by God for Israel. He was actually making reference to Jesus because in Stephen's defense, in the book of Acts, chapter seven, he revealed that Jesus was the prophet that Moses spoke about that was a prophet like unto him.

Acts 7:37

It was this [very] Moses who said to the children of Israel, God will raise up for you a Prophet from among your brethren as He raised me up. (AMP)

It means that just in the same way Israel looked unto Moses for every aspect of their provision and livelihood, New Testament believers will have to look unto Jesus Christ for same. For the entire Bible is written to reveal a Person.

If the Bible was written to reveal a Person, it is because everything that pertains to our lives as believers, we seek and receive from that Person. It is the ministry of that Person that is designed to bring about our sufficiency in life and destiny. This means that the only way God has made to resolve all our needs, is by showing us that Person, Jesus. In God's presence, Jesus is revealed.

Philippians 4:19
But my God shall supply all your need according to his riches in glory by Christ Jesus. (KJV)

This is what the word *"doctrine"* means in the New Testament. A close study of Scriptures reveals that the doctrine of God is not plural, but singular. Any time you find the word "doctrine" in plural it is either doctrines of men or doctrines of devils. God has only one *'Doctrine'*, and His Name is Jesus.

Mark 7:7
*In vain (fruitlessly and without profit) do they worship Me, ordering and teaching [to be obeyed] as **doctrines** the commandments and precepts of men. (AMP)*

Colossians 2:22
*Referring to things all of which perish with being used. To do this is to follow human precepts and **doctrines**. (AMP)*

1 Timothy 4:1

*BUT THE [Holy] Spirit distinctly and expressly declares that in latter times some will turn away from the faith, giving attention to deluding and seducing spirits and **doctrines** that demons teach, (AMP)*

1 Timothy 4:1
*Now the Spirit speaketh expressly, that in the latter times some shall depart from the faith, giving heed to seducing spirits, and **doctrines** of devils; (KJV)*

God's *Doctrine is* singular because it points to the Person. Therefore, the content of our messages should be about that one Person; Jesus Christ.

Hebrews 6:1
*Therefore leaving the principles of the **doctrine** of Christ, let us go on unto perfection; not laying again the foundation of repentance from dead works, and of faith toward God, (KJV)*

2 John 1:9
Whosoever transgresseth, and abideth not in the doctrine of Christ, hath not God. He that abideth in the doctrine of Christ, he hath both the Father and the Son. (KJV)

Hence, if we don't want to be similar to seducing spirits, devils and demons in having more than one doctrine, our lives must reflect only one Doctrine, Jesus.

The Preeminence of Jesus the Christ

Going through the book of Colossians chapter 1, we see Jesus unveiled.

Colossians 1:12-20

12. Giving thanks unto the Father, which hath made us meet to be partakers of the inheritance of the saints in light:

13. Who hath delivered us from the power of darkness, and hath translated [us] into the kingdom of his dear Son:

14. In whom we have redemption through his blood, [even] the forgiveness of sins:

15. Who is the image of the invisible God, the firstborn of every creature:

16. For by him were all things created, that are in heaven, and that are in earth, visible and invisible, whether [they be] thrones, or dominions, or principalities, or powers: all things were created by him, and for him:

17. And he is before all things, and by him all things consist.

18. And he is the head of the body, the church: who is the beginning, the firstborn from the dead; that in all [things] he might have the preeminence.

19. For it pleased [the Father] that in him should all fulness dwell;

20. And, having made peace through the blood of his cross, by him to reconcile all things unto himself; by him, [I say], whether [they be] things in earth, or things in heaven. (KJV)

God deals with us as citizens in the Kingdom of His dear Son. In this Jesus, the Bible says we have redemption through His Blood and even the forgiveness of sin. This same Jesus is the image of the invisible God. Do you know what that means? It means when you see Jesus, you have seen God.

This same Jesus is the firstborn of every creature. Thus, he existed before all things. All things were created by Him and for Him. It is because of Him that you were created. Please take some time to study the book of Colossians and underline words like, *"in Christ"*, *"for Christ"*, *"through Christ"*, and *"by Christ"*. You will be amazed.

The book of Colossians says that it is by Him and for Him that you and I were created. It means we have no meaning without Him and no meaning outside of Him. If you have not met Him, you don't know yourself yet. Only at the instance of Peter meeting Jesus, and him catching a revelation of the Christ, did Jesus disclose who Peter was.

Matthew 16:18
And I say also unto thee, That thou art Peter, and upon this rock I will build my church; and the gates of hell shall not prevail against it. (KJV)

Matthew 16:19
And I will give unto thee the keys of the kingdom of heaven: and whatsoever thou shalt bind on earth shall be bound in heaven: and whatsoever thou shalt loose on earth shall be loosed in heaven. (KJV)

"Just one passion; Just one purpose,
Is to know You more and more.
When I know You, I will find me.

Chapter Ten – Christ Revealed in His Presence

*No life outside You; No one beside You,
Let me know You more and more.
When I know You I will find me".*
— *Dunsin Oyekan*

It is the revelation of Jesus Christ that gives us an indication of our identity, purpose and essence in life. Everything is built around this Personality, and the office He administers in the Heavenlies. This is the good news of the Gospel. This Personality is revealed from the book of Genesis to Revelation.

Our doctrine is the Person that the Bible is about, and His Kingdom administration; Jesus Christ, the Son of the Living God.

Matthew 6:25-33

25. Therefore I say unto you, Take no thought for your life, what ye shall eat, or what ye shall drink; nor yet for your body, what ye shall put on. Is not the life more than meat, and the body than raiment?
26. Behold the fowls of the air: for they sow not, neither do they reap, nor gather into barns; yet your heavenly Father feedeth them. Are ye not much better than they?
27. Which of you by taking thought can add one cubit unto his stature?

28. And why take ye thought for raiment? Consider the lilies of the field, how they grow; they toil not, neither do they spin:

29. And yet I say unto you, That even Solomon in all his glory was not arrayed like one of these.

30. Wherefore, if God so clothe the grass of the field, which to day is, and to morrow is cast into the oven, [shall he] not much more [clothe] you, O ye of little faith?

31. Therefore take no thought, saying, What shall we eat? or, What shall we drink? or, Wherewithal shall we be clothed?

32. (For after all these things do the Gentiles seek:) for your heavenly Father knoweth that ye have need of all these things.

33. But seek ye first the kingdom of God, and his righteousness; and all these things shall be added unto you. (KJV)

From the above Scripture, we see that Jesus personally discourages us as Christians, from running after things that unbelievers (Gentiles) are doomed to run after. You know what happens when our pursuit is for material things, we will collide with mammon, and mammon possesses our souls.

Consequently, mammon goes on to give us a new interpretation of life, a new drive and a new vision that is definitely off God's course. God forbids. Do you need comfort, prosperity, lifting and promotion? All these are built into your service of Jesus. Most of us think that apart from Jesus, we need something else. Meanwhile, the Bible says that we are complete in Him.

Colossians 2:10
And ye are complete in him, which is the head of all principality and power: (KJV)

The only One we need to seek is Jesus Christ. We are not called to look for money, but to follow Jesus Christ. Jesus will tell us where money is; for He is the Way. He knows the way to everything in heaven and on earth. He knows we have need of these things but His prescription for life is to seek first the Kingdom of God and His righteousness (not self-righteousness), and then the things that the Gentiles seek, will navigate in our direction.

If you have been taught, or you are teaching prosperity any other way than this, what you are preaching is an error. It means that you have removed Christ from the equation. An error is a doctrine that is devoid of Christ as the pivot. The Bible is a revelation of a Person. Our ministry is to teach the people under our surveillance, about Jesus, and to lose them to Jesus. A good New Testament minister loses his members to Jesus. If what you are doing is designed to tie the people to yourself, then you are working at cross purposes with Jesus; and just in case He needs to free His Church, He may have to drop you.

Luke 17:2

It would be better for him if a millstone were hung around his neck, and he were thrown into the sea, than that he should offend one of these little ones. (NKJV)

For by Jesus do all things consist. Thus, the meaning of anything is not known except we ask Him. Our call as Christians is to pursue Jesus. When you see a man that doesn't have Christ as the center of his life, family, ministry and everything he does, such a man is evil.

Psalm 5:4

For You are not a God who takes pleasure in wickedness, Nor shall evil dwell with You. (NKJV)

Prayer Point

Father in the name of Jesus, arise O Lord into Your proper place of honor and glory, above our ambitions, and above our likes and dislikes. Let us sink, that You may rise above all that concerns us. In Jesus' most holy Name we pray, Amen.

CHAPTER ELEVEN

Our Walk with Christ

Luke 11:34

The light of the body is the eye: therefore when thine eye is single, thy whole body also is full of light; but when [thine eye] is evil, thy body also [is] full of darkness. (KJV)

In walking with Christ, we need a single eye. This means we must make Him our unique goal. Being single-eyed means following Him, His method, strategy and voice, in all we do. If we do not have a single eye, the Bible does not say we have a double eye, it says we are evil. When Christ is taken out of the equation, we are left with Satan.

Very subtly and unconsciously, we begin to operate the principles of Satan; his strategy. We may still think we are standing in Christ, but we have fallen into error.

1 Corinthians 10:12

Therefore let him who thinks he stands take heed lest he fall. (NKJV)

If we remove Jesus from the equation, we are left with darkness; and a lot of believers do not know that they are serving darkness. You want disciples that will last? People that receive Jesus and abide? Point them to Jesus. If they are exposed to the Gospel of Christ; the Gospel of the Kingdom, they will abide. The moment they see the King, their journey in life and destiny begins. Their hearts become the headquarters of God; the entry point of God into the earth.

The ark of God was the center of the civilization for the Jews, as they travelled through the wilderness, to the promised-land. Their camping methods were consistent with reverence to the ark. The ark was the heart of their civilization, as Christ is the ark of our civilization as Christians. We live for Him. It is in Him that we live, move and have our being.

Acts 17:28
For in Him we live and move and have our being; as even some of your [own] poets have said, For we are also His offspring. (AMP)

He supplies the energy that takes us about our daily activities. It is by the inspiration of His Spirit that we can speak for Him. That is why a Christian is not called to be creative, but to yield. The agenda that will come through every vessel is already known. We simply follow Him, trusting that He knows the way through the wilderness. Everything he does is in our best interest, to destroy any idol that may have the capacity to take our hearts in the days to come.

Our dignity and respect as children of God, does not come from the amount of money we have, the exotic cars we drive, or the mansions we live in. All these can be distractions to the Church, if Jesus is not at the center.

How much of Jesus do we carry? How much of Him do we have in our plans, businesses, careers, strategies, ministries and families. The meaning of everything is inside of Him. Please don't get us wrong, Christ is not against prosperity. In fact, He became poor that we might be rich.

2 Corinthians 8:9

For you are becoming progressively acquainted with and recognizing more strongly and clearly the grace of our Lord Jesus Christ (His kindness, His gracious generosity, His undeserved favor and spiritual blessing), [in] that though He was [so very] rich, yet for your sakes He became [so very] poor, in order that by His poverty you might become enriched (abundantly supplied). (AMP)

However, there is pathway to wealth and abundance. If we don't follow the protocol of the Kingdom, we will end up serving mammon.

Matthew 6:24

No one can serve two masters; for either he will hate the one and love the other, or he will stand by and be devoted to the one and despise and be against the other. You cannot serve God and mammon (deceitful riches, money, possessions, or whatever is trusted in). (AMP)

We must truly surrender ourselves to Jesus, so that He will bring us out in better colors, than any effort of ours can ever bring out. Please my sister, marry the man that Jesus is recommending. He might be below your status right now, but I assure you that you will never regret God's choice. However, please be very sure that it is God's voice you heard. A positive confirmation with two or three prayer partners is highly recommended; for in the multitude of counselors, there is safety (Proverbs 11:14).

Do you have a love relationship with God? Does He know you?

Colossians 1:18

And he is the head of the body, the church: who is the beginning, the firstborn from the dead; that in all [things] he might have the preeminence. (KJV)

Is Jesus preeminent in your life? Is it true that the wisdom behind your life and all that you do is what Jesus tells you? The plans He has for you are better than the ones you have for yourself, or that which your ancestors had for you.

Philippians 1:21

For me to live is Christ [His life in me], and to die is gain [the gain of the glory of eternity]. (AMP)

This is Paul speaking in the above text. Paul's definition of living is living out the will of Christ, that is, the Christian life. It is only when we have lived for Christ that death becomes gain.

In Peter's speech on the day of Pentecost, he said a lot of political and historical things, which included the previous dealings of God. Therefore, the people he was addressing knew that he wasn't a novice. However, the true substance of his message, are in the verses below. All he did, was point to Jesus.

Acts 2:32-35
32. This Jesus hath God raised up, whereof we all are witnesses.
33. Therefore being by the right hand of God exalted, and having received of the Father the promise of the Holy Ghost, he hath shed forth this, which ye now see and hear.
34. For David is not ascended into the heavens: but he saith himself, The LORD said unto my Lord, Sit thou on my right hand,
35. Until I make thy foes thy footstool. (KJV)

Acts 2:36

Therefore let all the house of Israel know assuredly, that God hath made that same Jesus, whom ye have crucified, both Lord and Christ. (KJV)

No one could successfully preach any message in the Bible without mentioning Jesus the Christ. His Name was even mentioned in their salutations.

Galatians 1:3-4

Grace [be] to you and peace from God the Father, and [from] our Lord Jesus Christ, Who gave himself for our sins, that he might deliver us from this present evil world, according to the will of God and our Father: (KJV)

Ephesians 1:1-3

1. Paul, an apostle of Jesus Christ by the will of God, to the saints which are at Ephesus, and to the faithful in Christ Jesus:
2. Grace [be] to you, and peace, from God our Father, and [from] the Lord Jesus Christ.
3. Blessed [be] the God and Father of our Lord Jesus Christ, who hath blessed us with all spiritual blessings in heavenly [places] in Christ: (KJV)

Philippians 1:1-2

Paul and Timotheus, the servants of Jesus Christ, to all the saints in Christ Jesus which are at Philippi, with the bishops and deacons: Grace [be] unto you, and peace, from God our Father, and [from] the Lord Jesus Christ. (KJV)

Colossians 1:1-2

Paul, an apostle of Jesus Christ by the will of God, and Timotheus [our] brother, To the saints and faithful brethren in Christ which are at Colosse: Grace [be] unto you, and peace, from God our Father and the Lord Jesus Christ. (KJV)

1 Peter 1:1-2

Peter, an apostle of Jesus Christ, to the strangers scattered throughout Pontus, Galatia, Cappadocia, Asia, and Bithynia, Elect according to the foreknowledge of God the Father, through sanctification of the Spirit, unto obedience and sprinkling of the blood of Jesus Christ: Grace unto you, and peace, be multiplied. (KJV)

How come a pastor can preach for a whole year, and he never tells people about the Christ? How come we never teach the deep workings of Christ in the inner man, how to hear His voice, His dealings, how to yield to Him, and how to decrease, so that Jesus can increase?

The word "Christ" in the Bible refers to Jesus' heavenly ministry. There is a portfolio that He has in heaven, which is an administrative ministry that is given to Him by the Father. The office is called that of *"the Christ"*. It is both a ministry and an office.

Philip preached about the majesty of the Christ to the people.

Acts 8:5&12

5. Then Philip went down to the city of Samaria, and preached Christ unto them.(KJV)

12. But when they believed Philip preaching the things concerning the kingdom of God, and the name of Jesus Christ, they were baptized, both men and women. (KJV)

Philip preached Christ and the Kingdom of God. He spoke about the Name of Jesus. There is no way you can preach this way and your audience will doubt that your focal point is Jesus the Christ. In the early days, it was clear that they preached Jesus.

Christ the Administrator

During the 40 days He spent on earth after His resurrection, Jesus taught His disciples things that pertained to the Kingdom of God.

Acts 1:3
To whom also he shewed himself alive after his passion by many infallible proofs, being seen of them forty days, and speaking of the things pertaining to the kingdom of God: (KJV)

It is from His office as the Christ, that He administers the Kingdom of God. In the same vein, He is the administrator of our Christian lives. He gives us wisdom, speaks to us, passing our prayers on to the Father. Everything that has to do with the Kingdom of God and our individual lives as believers, is designed to be managed by that office.

Romans 8:34
Who is he who condemns? It is Christ who died, and furthermore is also risen, who is even at the right hand of God, who also makes intercession for us. (NKJV)

The modus operandi of Christ, prioritizes His Kingdom over all else. And as His faithful followers, we must operate the exact same way. Some people came to report Jesus to John the Baptist, and got a shocking response:

John 3:26-30

26. And they came unto John, and said unto him, Rabbi, he that was with thee beyond Jordan, to whom thou barest witness, behold, the same baptizeth, and all [men] come to him.

27. John answered and said, A man can receive nothing, except it be given him from heaven.

28. Ye yourselves bear me witness, that I said, I am not the Christ, but that I am sent before him.

29. He that hath the bride is the bridegroom: but the friend of the bridegroom, which standeth and heareth him, rejoiceth greatly because of the bridegroom's voice: this my joy therefore is fulfilled. He must increase, but I [must] decrease. (KJV)

Glory to Jesus our Bridegroom; it is in His presence that men of stature are built. What is stature? It is a position of favor which we have before God, because we have submitted ourselves to His discipline. When he disciplined us, we yielded. When he tried us and stretched us, we did not run away. We acknowledged that His hand was involved, and we yielded. This always produces favor; a connection with God such as the one Peter expressed in the following encounter:

Acts 3:2-8

2. And a certain man lame from his mother's womb was carried, whom they laid daily at the gate of the temple which is called Beautiful, to ask alms of them that entered into the temple;

3. Who seeing Peter and John about to go into the temple asked an alms.

4. And Peter, fastening his eyes upon him with John, said, Look on us.

5. And he gave heed unto them, expecting to receive something of them.

6. Then Peter said, Silver and gold have I none; but such as I have give I thee: In the name of Jesus Christ of Nazareth rise up and walk.

7. And he took him by the right hand, and lifted [him] up: and immediately his feet and ankle bones received strength.

8. And he leaping up stood, and walked, and entered with them into the temple, walking, and leaping, and praising God. (KJV)

In the above Scripture, Peter had no resource apart from his relationship with Jesus. And it was from the abundance of his resource in Christ, that he executed the miracle. That is what we mean by stature. My question for you is this, *"Do you have something with Jesus the Christ?"* If you do not have money now, do you still have something?

As God's children, we have something worth more than gold or silver in Jesus Christ. Consequently, many great things are happening in our lives. Men are raised this way. Jesus is revealed in the presence of God. Hallelujah!

Prayer Point

Father in the Name of Jesus, in great humility we bow before You, and we take upon ourselves Your Name and Your nature. In Jesus' Precious Name, Amen.

CHAPTER TWELVE

His Presence; A Place of Dealings

In His presence, God usually asks us to make commitments. Sometimes, He goes the hard way. For example, in dealing with our finances, He might run us dry to test our trust in Him. When we pass the finance test, He counts it unto us as righteousness.

Psalm 20:7
Some trust in and boast of chariots and some of horses, but we will trust in and boast of the name of the Lord our God. (AMP)

Then all forms of temptation may come our way, and He allows them because His grace is sufficient for us to overcome them. Bear in mind also, that the Lord tempts no one. We are simply lured by our own desires.

James 1:13-15

13. Let no one say when he is tempted, "I am tempted by God"; for God cannot be tempted by evil, nor does He Himself tempt anyone.
14. But each one is tempted when he is drawn away by his own desires and enticed.
15. Then, when desire has conceived, it gives birth to sin; and sin, when it is full-grown, brings forth death. s(NKJV)

2 Corinthians 12:9

And He said to me, "My grace is sufficient for you, for My strength is made perfect in weakness." Therefore most gladly I will rather boast in my infirmities, that the power of Christ may rest upon me. (NKJV)

As a preacher, doors of nations may begin to open unto you. You will be sitting at your desk doing the same things you used to, yet invitations are coming from far and near; invitations that you did not manipulate. When you go to those fields, another test starts, because you will see things you have never seen before. You will experience honor which you have never had before. At this point, it would be dangerous to think you have fully arrived.

Philippians 3:12
Not that I have now attained [this ideal], or have already been made perfect, but I press on to lay hold of (grasp) and make my own, that for which Christ Jesus (the Messiah) has laid hold of me and made me His own. (AMP)

If your heart goes out into the world, the door is opened for corruption to have free access into your life. In His presence, your heart is always tamed. We must make sure that every accolade, honor or grace, is about God.

How many of us can God trust with a million Dollars? Will we still remain with Jesus? Or will we become puffed up with pride? In God's presence, the flesh and its cravings are dealt with.

"I just want to be where You are, dwelling daily in Your presence.
I don't want to worship from afar, I just want to be with You.

I want to be where You are; dwelling in Your presence.
Feasting at Your table, surrounded by Your glory.
In Your presence, that's where I always long to be.
I just want to be; I just want to be with You.

- Don Moen

In His presence, transformation takes place. Not only a change of heart from sin or evil, but a transformation into the image and likeness of God. It is a two-way thing. God can transform you from sin, so that He destroys the appetite for sin, iniquity, transgressions and trespass in you. He can also transform you by creating a godly appetite within you.

Discipline Versus Appetite

Discipline serves us as believers, to a very large extent. Without it, we would never have a consistent prayer life, for example. Discipline helps us create a foundation for consistency in our walk with God.

Proverbs 6:23

For sound advice is a beacon, good teaching is a light, moral discipline is a life path. (MSG)

However, though it helps to start from the place of discipline, the next higher level is that of a hunger and appetite for God.

Discipline is very strong but not as strong as appetite. A godly appetite is stronger than discipline. By discipline, you can choose to fast and pray for seven (7) days but given same circumstances, an appetite or hunger for God makes you go for twenty-one (21) days, without feeling it.

John 4:32

But He assured them, I have food (nourishment) to eat of which you know nothing and have no idea. (AMP)

This hunger and appetite for God, is beyond human comprehension. For men like John Knox, it is not just discipline that transformed their lives, but their appetite for God and His Kingdom. This hunger made him cry unto God saying, *"Give me Scotland or I die"*. When an appetite for God is formed in us, our satisfaction comes from the Holy Ghost.

A demon-possessed person can be prayed for, and the demon is cast out. However, there is a protocol that has been created in the brain; a physiological process already at work, which the victim may struggle with until a higher power intervenes, and restores his soul.

Psalm 23:3 (Paraphrase)
He restores my soul. (NKJV)

The transformation process is natural in God's presence. God begins to work out definite operation within you, and you grow from glory to glory.

2 Corinthians 3:18
But we all, with unveiled face, beholding as in a mirror the glory of the Lord, are being transformed into the same image from glory to glory, just as by the Spirit of the Lord. (NKJV)

We are not changed by discipline, but by the Spirit of God. A man who wants to see progressive transformation in his life, must learn to constantly practice the presence of God.

Isaiah 40:31
But those who wait on the LORD Shall renew their strength; They shall mount up with wings like eagles,

They shall run and not be weary, They shall walk and not faint. (NKJV)

In God's presence, His abilities within you, and the workings of the Spirit on your inner man, begin to find expression. The more you are in there with Him, the more He rubs off on you. Moses was in His presence for forty (40) days. When he came down, his face was shining like the sun.

Exodus 34:29-30

29. Now it was so, when Moses came down from Mount Sinai (and the two tablets of the Testimony were in Moses' hand when he came down from the mountain), that Moses did not know that the skin of his face shone while he talked with Him.

30. So when Aaron and all the children of Israel saw Moses, behold, the skin of his face shone, and they were afraid to come near him. (NKJV)

Exodus 34:33-35

33. And when Moses had finished speaking with them, he put a veil on his face.

34. But whenever Moses went in before the LORD to speak with Him, he would take the veil off until he came

out; and he would come out and speak to the children of Israel whatever he had been commanded.
35. And whenever the children of Israel saw the face of Moses, that the skin of Moses' face shone, then Moses would put the veil on his face again, until he went in to speak with Him. (NKJV)

The presence of God is the greatest cure for human deficiencies. Most of the time, it is not counseling we need, but His presence. Even when a man is delivered from the influence of a demon, the only thing that keeps him perpetually delivered is staying filled with God.

Matthew 12:43-45

43. "When a defiling evil spirit is expelled from someone, it drifts along through the desert looking for an oasis, some unsuspecting soul it can bedevil. When it doesn't find anyone,
44. it says, 'I'll go back to my old haunt.' On return it finds the person spotlessly clean, but vacant.
45. It then runs out and rounds up seven other spirits more evil than itself and they all move in, whooping it up. That person ends up far worse off than if he'd never gotten cleaned up in the first place. "That's what this

generation is like: You may think you have cleaned out the junk from your lives and gotten ready for God, but you weren't hospitable to my kingdom message, and now all the devils are moving back in." (MSG)

That is why if you detach from the presence of God, you will start doing again, those things which God already delivered you from. What keeps you constantly above principalities and powers is your ability to stay in His presence.

A typical scenario, is when for example, the Lord delivers a man from sexual immorality. God worked so much on his soul, that he hardly notices when a woman passes by. Then suddenly, one day at work, he begins to notice every lady that passes; what they are wearing, even to the slit on their skirts. This is a signal that he is shifting. He must run back to the secret place of God, as we all must.

"Then I will run to You; To Your words of truth.
It's not by might; Not by power,
But by the Spirit of God.
Yes, I will run the race; Till I see Your face.

> *So let me live in the glory of Your ways".*
> *- Alvin Slaughter*

His presence changes us into people of character. What is character? Why do we call the letters of the alphabet, characters? Because the alphabet "A" is always "A". Letter "S" is "S" at 9am in the morning or 9pm at night. "L" is still "L", whether in Europe or in India. They do not change, that is why we call them characters. Numbers are called characters because they do not change.

Character is something that does not change. Character makes you become committed to a set of values, without compromise. For example, if you value your marriage vows, you will never commit adultery, nor maltreat your spouse either verbally or physically. People who cheat on their spouses do not value their marriage vows.

As a person of character, there is no excuse in life for breaking your values and standards. For you, honesty is your only policy. You know that your future depends on your character, not your charisma. The life of a man of character is so integrated that his words, deeds and actions are one. What are you doing right now in secret that you should not be doing? Who are you with that you shouldn't be with?

A man of character is one with himself. The root word for *"holy"* in the Hebrew language is the word *"one"*. The Hebrew concept of holiness is integrity. That means being one. The number one confession in the Bible about God is, *"the Lord our God is one"*. If you walk up to a Jewish Rabbi, and ask him what the most important confession in the Bible is, here is what he will tell you:

Deuteronomy 6:4
Hear, O Israel: The LORD our God [is] one LORD: (KJV)

What does this mean? It means God is holy. Holiness means you are integrated; you are not more than one person. You are not a different person on Friday, than you are on Sunday in church. You are one. You are not multi-personality. When the Bible tells you to be holy, it is telling you to be one. Before you can have dominion in life, your character must be one. God gave man character before dominion. His image is His character.

Genesis 1:26

And God said, Let us make man in our image, after our likeness: and let them have dominion over the fish of the sea, and over the fowl of the air, and over the cattle, and over all the earth, and over every creeping thing that creepeth upon the earth. (KJV)

Is there any character in your life that you are finding difficult to let go? Enter His presence, and His light will burn off all filthiness out of your life. Men of character are made and sustained in His presence.

A Christian is secretly pure to God;
A Christian is righteously strict to himself;
A Christian is mercifully kind to others.
Is this you?

Prayer Point

Father in the Name of Jesus, please show us how to die to self, that we may rise again to newness of life in You. In Jesus Holy Name, Amen.

CHAPTER THIRTEEN

An Environment, Not a Location

"THE PRESENCE OF GOD IS AN "ENVIRONMENT", NOT A "LOCATION".

Genesis 2:8

And the LORD God planted a garden eastward in Eden; and there he put the man whom he had formed. (KJV)

God made plants and domiciled them in the earth, so that they will receive their nutrients and sustainability from the resources that are in the ground. Similarly, the location where He put man became his habitat; man's dwelling place.

Genesis 2:15-17

15. And the LORD God took the man, and put him into the garden of Eden to dress it and to keep it.

16. And the LORD God commanded the man, saying, Of every tree of the garden thou mayest freely eat:

17. But of the tree of the knowledge of good and evil, thou shalt not eat of it: for in the day that thou eatest thereof thou shalt surely die. (KJV)

Man had two assignments in the garden; to dress and keep the garden. Note that it wasn't stated in the Bible that God visited any other region of Eden except the Garden. The garden was like an embassy; like a part of heaven that was present on the earth.

The moment you walk into the British embassy in Abuja, which is the capital city of Nigeria, West Africa, you are no longer on Nigerian soil. According to diplomatic laws, you are in Britain. Anything that you do there, will be judged according to the laws of Britain because that is a part of Britain, in another land.

The Garden of Eden was actually a very good picture of what we call a temple. A temple is a natural location where you encounter a supernatural being. The Garden of Eden was a natural location but the infrastructure that was built into it was such that you could touch natural things and still experience supernatural things.

In Exodus 25, the layout of the temple was built to capture natural and supernatural offices. The temple was built to capture the offices of men, that of the angels, and the office of God. It was a strange kind of layout. The table of shew bread was designed in such a way that human priests could minister there.

In the Holy of Holies, we find the two golden cherubim, representing the office of the cherubim in heaven, as well as the mercy seat, representing the office of God. The Garden of Eden was also built according to specific dimensions. We say this because God could conveniently step into the garden without any disruption between the realms of heaven and earth.

It was a merger between the natural and the supernatural. It was compatible for both God and man; both enjoying encounters in the supernatural. The garden was designed to inhabit God's presence.

Psalm 16:11

You will show me the path of life; In Your presence is fullness of joy; At Your right hand are pleasures forevermore. (NKJV)

The proof of God's presence is joy unspeakable.

1 Peter 1:7-8

7. That the trial of your faith, being much more precious than of gold that perisheth, though it be tried with fire, might be found unto praise and honour and glory at the appearing of Jesus Christ:
8. Whom having not seen, ye love; in whom, though now ye see [him] not, yet believing, ye rejoice with joy unspeakable and full of glory: (KJV)

Anytime your experience is exactly as described in the above Scriptures, it is an indication that you are in the presence of God. This Lord that you have so defended, for Whom you have gone through so many trials, even without seeing Him with your physical eyes; yet you are full of faith, believing Him, and you are filled with joy unspeakable.

Peter's emphasis is that, though you cannot see God with your physical eyes, His presence is evident when there is joy in your spirit.

Happiness on the other hand, is as a result of happenings. For example, you are happy on the day you get married, have a baby, or get a new job.

Joy is spiritual, and cannot be understood. It is not a product of circumstances. Joy is the evidence of the fact that your spirit is alive, and is able to tap into the frequencies of God's presence.

Have you ever experienced this feeling? Then you are blessed indeed. The Bible says that, the joy of the Lord which rises in our spirits, is actually a sign of strength.

Nehemiah 8:10
Then [Ezra] told them, Go your way, eat the fat, drink the sweet drink, and send portions to him for whom nothing is prepared; for this day is holy to our Lord. And be not grieved and depressed, for the joy of the Lord is your strength and stronghold. (AMP)

True children of God, who have found intimacy with Him, wake up most of the time with a floodgate of joy from within. They don't know why, neither can they explain the reason for this much joy. Mundane challenges still stare them in the face, and the situations have not been altered in any way. But something beyond their circumstances is responsible for this flood in their hearts. That is why the Bible calls it joy unspeakable, full of weight of glory. It is beyond mental comprehension and is a true gift from God.

John 16:33

These things I have spoken to you, that in Me you may have peace. In the world you will have tribulation; but be of good cheer, I have overcome the world." (NKJV)

And if the devil wants to ensure that he distracts you from the presence of God, he does something to punctuate that joy.

The presence of God is environmental, not locational. When your spirit enters into that environment, there comes a release of joy. Meanwhile, you can be in the same location with someone in the natural, but you are not in the same environment in the spirit. You might be so full of joy, while the person is full of depression. Same location, different environments.

You are both interacting with different entities in these environments. He is interacting with the spirit that brings depression and hopelessness but you are in another environment that is feeding your spirit with life, which is responsible for the surge of joy.

Peter described people that were earnestly intimate with Jesus so much so, that trials lacked the power and authority to shift their alignment. They had not seen Jesus physically, yet they believed in Him enough to rejoice in the midst of their trials.

Psalm 16:11
Thou wilt shew me the path of life: in thy presence [is] fulness of joy; at thy right hand [there are] pleasures for evermore. (KJV)

Accessing God's Environment

God's environment in this context, refers to the conscious manifest presence of God; not the omnipresence of God that makes Him present everywhere at the same time.

It is important to note that it is not all the time that we hear God speak. Sometimes, there can be seasons of silence, and it is not because we are spiritually down but it is God who decides these things. This period of silence might even occur during active fasting and prayers, yet, there is no release of His presence in your spirit. Because of the lack of the release, though we are spiritually agile, we are not able to enter into the economy of heaven's disclosures.

Therefore, we must value every revelation we receive from God's throne. Whenever you notice access (an opening) of your spirit into heavenly activity, you have stepped into the environment strictly by God's ordination. It is He that draws you in.

Song of Solomon 1:4
Draw me, we will run after thee: the king hath brought me into his chambers: we will be glad and rejoice in thee, we will remember thy love more than wine: the upright love thee. (KJV)

The Spirit of the Lord is in your spirit because you are regenerated. This means you have unlimited potential, for access into God's environment.

Psalm 51:11

Cast me not away from thy presence; and take not thy holy spirit from me. (KJV)

The implication of God casting you away, is that He withdraws His Spirit, so you can no longer have access to His presence.

The Government of His Presence

Genesis 2:15

15. And the LORD God took the man, and put him into the garden of Eden to dress it and to keep it.
16. And the LORD God commanded the man, saying, Of every tree of the garden thou mayest freely eat:
17. But of the tree of the knowledge of good and evil, thou shalt not eat of it: for in the day that thou eatest thereof thou shalt surely die. (KJV)

God did not give Adam instructions outside of the garden. God gave man instructions within the garden because the garden metaphorically captured a picture of His presence. Another evidence of God's presence is His government.

For example, if somebody offends me and I take it to God in prayer, His response will most likely be this Scripture;

1 Peter 5:7
Casting the whole of your care [all your anxieties, all your worries, all your concerns, once and for all] ons Him, for He cares for you affectionately and cares about you watchfully. (AMP)

This Scripture serves as God's direct instruction concerning my issue. It is His governmental ruling about my prayer point. Therefore, I must obey Him and take my mind off the offence, knowing that His judgement is perfect. In God's presence, we find the manifestation of His eternal government.

Genesis 2:16-17
16. And the Lord God commanded the man, saying, You may freely eat of every tree of the garden;
17. But of the tree of the knowledge of good and evil and blessing and calamity you shall not eat, for in the day that you eat of it you shall surely die. (AMP)

This is His government. The presence of God is not a feeling. It is a place where the government and dominion of God rules; where the Holy Spirit has all the liberty to express Himself. In His presence, the dominion mandate is expressed. That is why there is perfect law and order in heaven. When Satan attempted to bring disorder, he was thrown out of heaven.

Isaiah 14:12-13

12. "How you are fallen from heaven, O Lucifer, son of the morning! How you are cut down to the ground, You who weakened the nations!

13. For you have said in your heart: 'I will ascend into heaven, I will exalt my throne above the stars of God; I will also sit on the mount of the congregation On the farthest sides of the north; (NKJV)

As Adam and Eve violated the heavenly order in the garden of Eden, they were thrown out.

Genesis 3:22-24

22. Then the LORD God said, "Behold, the man has become like one of Us, to know good and evil. And now, lest he put out his hand and take also of the tree of life, and eat, and live forever"—

*23. therefore the LORD God sent him out of the garden of Eden to till the ground from which he was taken.
24. So He drove out the man; and He placed cherubim at the east of the garden of Eden, and a flaming sword which turned every way, to guard the way to the tree of life. (NKJV)*

The same way we bore the image of Adam, we must bear the image of God. Therefore, a man that bears the image of God is truly within the environment of God.

1 Corinthians 15:48-49
*48. As [is] the earthy, such [are] they also that are earthy: and as [is] the heavenly, such [are] they also that are heavenly.
49. And as we have borne the image of the earthy, we shall also bear the image of the heavenly. (KJV)*

Prayer Point

Father in the Name of Jesus, please cause us to always come boldly to Your presence, that we may enjoy fellowship with You, and all the blessings attached therewith. In Jesus' Name, Amen.

CHAPTER FOURTEEN

In His Presence

*"Are you hungry enough for His presence?
Make room in your heart for Him."*

Much of what we do as Christians today, is often in the flesh. We label it as spiritual, but even God knows it really isn't. When we pray, are we truly praying? Because other religions pray, even more than us Christians. Religious people pray all the time, going from one prayer retreat to another, yet we see no change. Many of them don't even know the Lord, yet they pray. Traditional priests and herbalists pray, even those of the occult pray.

The point here is that there is no power in only prayers. It is the presence of God that makes all the difference. When we commune with the Lord, there is power. It is in practicing the presence of the Lord that we tap into realms of God's power. Empty words and vain repetitions don't move God.

Matthew 6:7
And when you pray, do not use vain repetitions as the heathen do. For they think that they will be heard for their many words. (NKJV)

Only in the realm of the spirit do we see results. There are no results in the flesh. People pray, fast and even praise in the flesh, with no result. You can say the Name of Jesus till you are blue in the face, and nothing will happen until the presence of God shows up. People are generally slack in detecting the right realm. Unfortunately, professing Christians are not exempted. Countless times, we have wrongly assumed that an emotional service, was Holy Ghost filled. Meanwhile, He was far from being present.

Many of us are trying to turn on our engines by ourselves, and it is not working because there is no profit in the flesh.

John 6:63
It is the spirit that quickeneth; the flesh profiteth nothing: the words that I speak unto you, [they] are spirit, and [they] are life. (KJV)

The secret place is where God wants us to be, and a lot of believers don't know how to get there. We must dwell in His secret place until the presence of God becomes our address. In that place, Jesus becomes 'realer' than our diseases, circumstances, sins, pains, fear, worries and sorrows.

Only few of God's children enjoy the fullness of their salvation. Many think of their destination but neglect the journey. The day-to-day experience of God's presence is something totally strange to many Christians but God expects us to experience Him daily.

Psalm 63:1
O God, You are my God; Early will I seek You; My soul thirsts for You; My flesh longs for You In a dry and thirsty land Where there is no water. (NKJV)

In the Old Testament, Enoch so walked with God that the things of the world grew strangely dim; just as an airplane lifts up into the sky, and the earth gets smaller and smaller until you can hardly see it.

Genesis 5:24
And Enoch walked [in habitual fellowship] with God; and he was not, for God took him [home with Him].
(AMP)

As a man experiences the conscious manifest presence of God, he begins to lose interest in the mundane things of this world. All of those things he once cherished and thought he could not do without, no longer have his interest. Why? He has encountered something far greater in God's presence. If we can apply simple discipline in our daily lives, we will see a marvelous improvement in our spiritual walk with God.

As Christians, we have something going on in our lives every day and night, all week long. We often do things just because we are used to doing them, or we follow the herd, just because others are doing it. These things, if not properly checked, can hinder our experience of God's conscious, manifest presence, in our everyday life.

Right now, we are not talking about sinful acts, but seemingly important things, that subtly hinder us from pressing into the presence of God. What is needed today, is spiritual discernment along with the boldness and courage to identify these things, and root them out once and for all.

If someone important was coming to visit you, wouldn't you cancel everything, and make preparations to receive your guest? Let us make room for our Lord who is not just a guest, but rather, an ultimate companion in our everyday walk

I pray that God in His goodness will bring us into a deep experience of Him, as we seek Him with all our hearts, in Jesus' Mighty Name, Amen.

Daily Expectation of God's Presence

I wonder how many Christians really have within their spirits, the daily expectation of God's presence.

How many truly expect a personal encounter with God?

Jeremiah 29:13

Then you will seek Me, inquire for, and require Me [as a vital necessity] and find Me when you search for Me with all your heart. (AMP)

Proverbs 8:17

I love those who love me, and those who seek me early and diligently shall find me. (AMP)

It is important to cultivate a daily expectation of God's presence. Each day presents a new opportunity to experience God, and fellowship with Him. Nothing more should occupy the mind of a Christian than discovering God daily, in every aspect of life.

A mother carries her child for nine months in expectation of a baby; that bundle of joy that will change everything about her life. Start your day seeking God's presence and expect to find Him in the gracious and glorious encounters throughout the day.

Practicing Stillness

The discipline of stillness is rare because we live in a noisy world. Stillness is perhaps one of the most difficult in our spiritual discipline.

Psalm 40:1
I waited patiently for the LORD; and he inclined unto me, and heard my cry. (KJV)

In the place of prayer, when you are done with your prayer list, learn to wait patiently for Him. Be still before Him, long enough for God to quicken you.

Psalm 40:2
He brought me up also out of an horrible pit, out of the miry clay, and set my feet upon a rock, [and] established my goings. (KJV)

Next, Psalm 40:3 takes place.

Psalm 40:3
And he hath put a new song in my mouth, [even] praise unto our God: many shall see [it], and fear, and shall trust in the LORD. (KJV)

He will put a new song in your mouth, and you will start to sing melodious songs on your own. The realm of the Spirit begins with a melody. As you get deeper in the spirit, you begin to sway and even your body becomes light like a feather. Then suddenly your tongues, that heavenly language, becomes precise and distinct, you are not just blabbing.

Something suddenly happens, and this happens when you are in the practice of His presence. Jesus Christ becomes more real to you than life. Sometimes, God does not mind if you play a worship song to change the atmosphere around you, before you get in to the Spirit.

Please take note that you do not need music to get into the Spirit but our environment needs it because we can get distracted by things. Worship helps us connect, and helps us forget our troubles so that we can fully focus on Him. In here it is all about Jesus.

The Tabernacle in Practice

For easy understanding, we will use the tabernacle of Moses to explain the seven manifestations of the practice of the Lord's presence.

1. You enter through the gate. At the gate Jesus becomes real.

2. The brazen altar; the altar of sacrifice, the cross and the Blood of Jesus Christ, becomes more real than any bondage of sin and shame. There is brokenness, repentance, cleansing, and forgiveness. Old things are passed away and the very memory of sin disappears from our souls. A lot of people confess their sins in the flesh, and that is why they go back to sin again. Brethren when you repent in the spirit, it is difficult for you to go back to your sinful ways, because they have been erased by the Holy Ghost, right in His presence.

3. The third place is the bronze laver, which is the basin of water used by the priests to wash. This represents the Word of God. Here, the Word of God becomes real, powerful and effective. It is in this place that you take hold of God's Word with authority and power, and it becomes yours. Because you are in His presence, you experience the supernatural confidence that Saint John spoke about:

> ***1 John 5:14***
> *And this is the confidence that we have in him, that, if we ask any thing according to his will, he heareth us:*
> *(KJV)*

You are certain that He has heard you because you are in His presence. On the contrary, if you are in the flesh, you will doubt that God really heard you.

4. At the lampstand in the holy place, the will of God is revealed, and you know what exactly to do. His plans for you and His will, becomes your will.

5. At the table of the shewbread, your body is surrendered as a living sacrifice; the bread is your body. This is where we yield all our members as instruments of righteousness, offered as a living sacrifice, holy and acceptable unto Him. The greatest experience in the baptism of the Holy Spirit, is when we give him our bodies as living sacrifices, and our bodies become His body.

6. The altar of incense. This is where the Holy Spirit is represented. You cannot worship in the flesh; true worship comes from the Spirit.

John 4:24

God [is] a Spirit: and they that worship him must worship [him] in spirit and in truth. (KJV)

And as you worship in the spirit, you are in union and communion with the Master. Worship is intimacy with the Lord. In this place, the Lord takes hold of you, and every cell in your body adores Him, while every part of you magnifies His Name. It is not mental but spiritual; deep calling unto deep. Such depth in the spirit, deeply immersed in the presence of the Lord. Oh! what a place to be, where worship will explode inside of your being.

7. Lastly, the most holy place, the Holy of holies, is where you hear His voice. The place of the Ark of the

Covenant. This most sacred item in the tabernacle is kept here. The mercy seat, God's very throne is represented in the Holy of holies.

The late Karthyn Kulman of blessed memory would walk in to service without saying a word or praying, yet people were healed. How come this was happening without her saying a word or preaching a message? It is the manifest presence of God. When you have experienced the depth of His presence, He comes out with you, and your presence becomes His presence. You literally carry that glory as you come out. Your vessel has become His vessel.

The presence of God is the realm of the Spirit, where His promises are activated and victory comes to you. You cannot know the love of God except in His presence because in His presence, you fall in love with Jesus over and over again. It doesn't stop there; you are also given the capacity to love others.

Your eyes become His eyes; your touch becomes His touch; your voice becomes His voice; and with that, the world will know that Jesus is alive.

We are fully persuaded that nothing can separate us from the love of God.

Romans 8:35

Do you think anyone is going to be able to drive a wedge between us and Christ's love for us? There is no way! Not trouble, not hard times, not hatred, not hunger, not homelessness, not bullying threats, not backstabbing, not even the worst sins listed in Scripture: (MSG)

Romans 8:38-39

For I am persuaded beyond doubt (am sure) that neither death nor life, nor angels nor principalities, nor things impending and threatening nor things to come, nor powers, Nor height nor depth, nor anything else in all creation will be able to separate us from the love of God which is in Christ Jesus our Lord. (AMP)

Time must be given to cultivating silence before His presence, and this takes practice and discipline. We guarantee you that it is not easy, because there are strong and valid voices, calling us away from God to do "important things". Coming before God in quietness and waiting upon Him in silence, can accomplish more than days and weeks of feverish activities. For in His presence is fullness of joy, and at His right hand are pleasures for evermore (Psalm 16:11). Stay silent in His presence. King David, under the influence of the Holy Spirit, understood this very well;

Psalm 46:10

Let be and be still, and know (recognize and understand) that I am God. I will be exalted among the nations! I will be exalted in the earth! (AMP)

In silence, we begin to see and really get to know God, as He desires to reveal Himself. How much of God do you know? God longs for you to know Him as He really is. Get ready to meet God again and again. We must overcome the mindset that says a moment of silence is a moment wasted. The discipline of silence is the price we have to pay to get to know God. God bless you. Amen.

Prayer Point

Father in the Name of Jesus Christ, beyond these pages, I seek You Lord and my Spirit pants for you Oh Living Word. Please, reveal Yourself to me just as you are. In Jesus' Precious Name I pray, Amen.

CHAPTER FIFTEEN

Practice His Presence

Our ability to Concentrate; The Mind.

Most believers today cannot concentrate on anything spiritual for a significant amount of time. But we can concentrate on television, social media, entertainment of all kinds, parties, games, and so on. To occupy a man with things other than spiritual, is the predominant agenda of the devil. Unfortunately, the devil has the cooperation of the world around us in achieving his goal, and he does not find much resistance.

Thus, by the help of the Holy Spirit we must shun the world and its pleasure and all its distractions.

How to Practice His Presence

1. Shun the flesh and the world.

We live in a fun generation. There is such a great impulse for entertainment and fun, that unless it is fun and entertaining, we would have none of it. Even some churches are built on the premise of entertainment and fun, even amongst people that have been set free by the power of God. Majority of believers are now driven into their personal and professional lives by lust and greed. This is most appalling.

Entertainment is a cheap substitute for the real experience of God. You need the help of the Holy Spirit to shun the world. Ask him to help you and He will.

John 14:26

But the Comforter (Counselor, Helper, Intercessor, Advocate, Strengthener, Standby), the Holy Spirit,

Whom the Father will send in My name [in My place, to represent Me and act on My behalf], He will teach you all things. And He will cause you to recall (will remind you of, bring to your remembrance) everything I have told you. (AMP)

Plead the Blood of Jesus over your mind, the moment you notice your mind craving for some sort of ungodly appetite and entertainment. Go on a retreat, go on a fast, and pray for God to remove those cravings and he will. By the help of the Holy Spirit, you can devise some ways to discipline yourself from the things of the world.

2. Enter His Presence with Worship and Thanksgiving

Psalm 100:1-5
1. MAKE A joyful noise to the Lord, all you lands!
2. Serve the Lord with gladness! Come before His presence with singing!
3. Know (perceive, recognize, and understand with approval) that the Lord is God! It is He Who has made

us, not we ourselves [and we are His]! We are His people and the sheep of His pasture.

4. Enter into His gates with thanksgiving and a thank offering and into His courts with praise! Be thankful and say so to Him, bless and affectionately praise His name!

5. For the Lord is good; His mercy and loving-kindness are everlasting, His faithfulness and truth endure to all generations. (AMP)

The Message translation of verse 4, puts it this way;

Psalm 100:4

Enter with the password: "Thank you!" Make yourselves at home, talking praise. Thank him. Worship him. (MSG)

Enter with the password: *"thank you"*. Enter with reverential awe in worship; cultivate a holy and healthy appreciation for the presence of your God. Worship Him in the beauty of holiness. Worship Him because He is infinite and eternal over all, and worthy above all. I worship him because:

* He is sovereign.

* He is before all things; The Alpha and Omega. He alone is Immortal (Colossians 1:17).

* He created all things both in heaven, on earth and beneath the earth; both visible and invisible (Colossians 1:16).

* He upholds all things, sustaining all things and holding them together, by the Word of His power (Hebrews 1:13).

* He is above all things (Ephesians 4:6).

* He is unlimited. He knows everything completely, before it happens (Isaiah 46:10).

* He can do all things; nothing is too difficult for Him, neither is anything impossible with Him (Luke 1:37).

* He accomplishes all things (Isaiah 14:24).

* He rules over all things. All power and strength are in His hands (1 Chronicles 29:11-12).

* He is in control of all things (Romans 8:28).

* He is the God that redeems the helpless from their enemies.

* He rescues from the shadow of death, because He is a good God.

* He heals our diseases.

* He protects us from the storms of life that threaten to sink us.

Worship Him, worship Him; that is your access into His presence.

Psalm 95:2
Let us come before his presence with thanksgiving, and make a joyful noise unto him with psalms. (KJV)

Psalm 100:1-2
Make a joyful noise unto the LORD, all ye lands. Serve the LORD with gladness: come before his presence with singing. (KJV)

Psalm 22:3
But thou [art] holy, [O thou] that inhabitest the praises of Israel. (KJV)

3. Meditate on God's Word; The Bible.

Meditation is eating, chewing and regurgitating the Word of God, so that it becomes part and parcel of our spirit and lives.

After you have worshipped Him and there is a release, open your Bible and begin to meditate on the Word of God. True meditation begins with the Word, for it leads us into the heart and mind of God. Approaching God's Word for anything less than meeting God, can be sacrilegious.

Many come to the Word to get Scriptures to argue or to prove a point, while others come to find Scriptural backing to establish a doctrine. This is quite wrong. We must so discipline ourselves to come to the Word with a holy expectation, to meet with God. We should meditate on His Word until we can feel the breath of God upon us. Just like David in Psalm 42:1. He knew how to pant after God.

And as we meditate on God's Word, our thoughts become clearer, making our minds clean sanctuaries, appropriate and pleasing for the Master's use. Very often, while mediating on God's Word, a verse or

Word will capture my attention, and in that verse or Word, will be an answer to the question in my heart.

4. Live in Obedience.

Obedience is not something that comes naturally to any of us, particularly in spiritual matters. There are many things arraigned against us in the world, and this makes it absolutely necessary to pay all diligence to obeying God's voice through His Word.

Though our salvation took place in one day, there is still the daily renewal of our walk with God that is paramount. Each day, we must diligently follow the leading of the Scriptures. One thing about the leading of the Holy Spirit is that, He does not lead us contrary to the clear and plain teaching of the Bible. This cannot be stressed enough.

The key to disciplining ourselves in the area of obedience, is to always keep in mind, to whom we are being obedient. And of course, the ultimate resolve of our obedience is to encounter God.

> *"Trust and obey;*
> *For there is no other way;*
> *To be happy in Jesus;*
> *But to trust and obey".*

The predominantly unhappy Christians in the Church today are those walking in disobedience. Practicing His presence involves total obedience to all that God instructs. I am confident that God in His goodness and mercy, will bring you and me into deeper experience of Himself as we seek Him with all of our hearts.

5. Drop Ungodly Relationships

Your friends will either make or break your deeper walk with Christ. Please carefully choose your friends in this regard. Although it is not necessary to be rude, but some friends need to be marginalized, to lessen the damage upon your inner life. Sometimes we are thrown in with friends that are carnal in nature and frivolous in life. It is impossible for our friends to distract us from our walk with Christ, and we still maintain a vibrant life of worship.

Many times, we will have to leave our friends behind in order to concentrate on our only true friend, Jesus. Please cultivate friendships with those who have made Christ their constant companion. These simple things will go a long way in maintaining a vibrant life of worship and praise.

Prayer Points

Father in the Name of Jesus, please dwell in our hearts without any rival. Rend the veil of our self-life from top to bottom, as You did the temple veil.

Father in the Name of Jesus, the world is very evil and we are running out of time. Oh Father, please lay hold of us and help us dwell in your presence daily. In Your most precious Name we pray, Amen.

CONCLUSION

The devil's Battle Cry

The battle cry of the devil is a kind of standing order for all demons, against the disciples of Jesus. It is an order that Satan has given to all his demons concerning you and me, and that is: *"Break the fellowship between man and his Lord".* When there is a report about a disciple troubling the kingdom of the darkness, the devil tells his demons to go and break the fellowship between that person and his Lord, by sin or disobedience. This is not new, as the devil has been using it from time immemorial. He succeeded in the Garden of Eden, he succeeded against the children of David, but he will fail woefully over your life in Jesus' Mighty Name!

Balak and Balaam

In Numbers chapter 22 through 25, the children of Israel were going to the Promised Land, and were conquering all the way. Any nation they faced, they destroyed totally. As they got to the land of a certain king called Barak, who had heard all that the children of Israel did to other kings, he took some brutal steps;

There was a certain prophet named Balaam. Whatever he spoke came to pass. So Balak the son of Zippor, king of the Moabites sent for Balaam the son of Beor, the great grandson of Abraham and Keturah, the wife Abraham had after the death of Sarah. He sent the elders of Moab and the elders of Midian with rewards of divination for him saying, *"behold there is a people that came out of Egypt, and they have covered the face of the earth. Now they have settled and abide over against me. Come now and curse them for they are too mighty for me. Curse them that I may prevail and smite them, and drive them out of the land; for I know that he whom you bless is blessed and he whom you curse is cursed. And you will be rewarded for this divination".*

Balaam said to God, *"shall I go?"* And God said, *"No! How can you go against my people?"* So, he sent word back to the king saying, *"Sorry, I am not coming"*. The king sent again, more honorable men than the first set, and Balaam asked God again. This time, God said, *"I have already told you not to go. But if you want to go, go".*

Balaam went and he demanded for seven altars to be built, and for seven oxen and seven rams to be prepared. The king provided all he demanded for the sacrifice. But when Balaam opened his mouth to curse Israel, instead of curses, blessings were flowing forth. This made Barak angry. He said to Balaam, *"I asked you to curse them, not to bless them"*. Balaam tried the second and third time, still blessings came forth. At this point, Barak had to say to him, *"listen; if you are not going to curse them, at least don't bless them"*. Then Balaam said concerning Israel;

Numbers 23:21

He hath not beheld iniquity in Jacob, neither hath he seen perverseness in Israel: the LORD his God [is] with him, and the shout of a king [is] among them. (KJV)

He continued, *"So I cannot curse them, because there is no enchantment or divination that can stand against Israel"*. Balaam also lifted up his eyes saw Israel abiding in their tents, according to their tribes. All well aligned, with no one breaking their ranks. He said:

Numbers 24:5

How goodly are thy tents, O Jacob, [and] thy tabernacles, O Israel! (KJV)

But before Balaam left Barak, he told him, *"Nobody can curse these people because God has blessed them. But let me teach you a method you can use to defeat them. If you can cause these people to go against their own God, if there can be separation between the two of them, if you can break the fellowship between them and their God, then you will not even need to fight them, they would be pitching themselves against their God"*.

So, the children of Israel were invited to a peace feast. Lots of eating, drinking, and sexual immorality took place.

Numbers 25:1

While the Israelites were camped at Acacia Grove, some of the men defiled themselves by having sexual relations with local Moabite women. (NLT)

The men of Israel looked upon the scantily dressed daughters of Moab. Gradually, they began to touch them. And before long, they were committing adultery with them. One of the children of Israel even brought Midianite woman into his family tent, flaunting his behavior in front of Moses.

Whom Phinehas the son Eleazar, the son of Aaron, killed with the woman with a javelin, thrusting both of them through the belly. For God had earlier warned them not to take a wife from among them.

Without Balak raising his sword, look at what happened. All he did was that he succeed in breaking the fellowship between the nation of Israel and their God. Therefore, when the fellowship between a man and his God is broken, because of sin, trouble comes. Is your fellowship with your God still intact? Are you dwelling in His presence?

Psalm 91:1

HE WHO dwells in the secret place of the Most High shall remain stable and fixed under the shadow of the Almighty [Whose power no foe can withstand]. (AMP)

Only then can he say;

Psalm 91:2-16 (Personalized)

2. The Lord is my refuge and my fortress, my God on him I lean, confidently trust and rely.

3. For then he will deliver me from the snare of the fowler and the deadly pestilence.

4. He will cover me with his wings and his truth and faithfulness are a shield for me.

5. I will not be afraid of evil plots and slanders of the wicked,

6. nor of sudden death that surprise at noonday.

7. A thousand may fall at my side, and ten thousand at my right hand, no harm will come near me.

8-12. No plague or calamity will come near my dwelling place for his angels have a charge over me and will keep me in all my ways. Their job is to keep me from falling.

13. I will tread upon the lion and the cobra. He will deliver me, he will set me on high because I am always in his presence, I have a personal knowledge of his love, mercy and kindness.

14-16. My God answers my prayers and he will satisfy me with long life, a life worth living with tranquility inward and outward and continuing through old age till death shall be mine. Amen and amen. Thank You Lord.

Numbers 25:9

And those that died in the plague were twenty and four thousand. (KJV)

If what we believe does not make God real to us, if what we believe does not make us more Christ-like in every aspect of our lives, of what value is it? Maintaining the conscious manifest presence of God in our lives is a responsibility we cannot shrink back from. May God grant us a desire for him that supersedes all other desires in Jesus Holy Name, Amen and Amen.

If you would like to give your life to Jesus, or you want to renew your relationship with Him, please say this prayer;

Lord Jesus, I come to Your throne of grace because I am tired of displeasing You with my life of sin. Please have mercy on me and show me Your salvation.

I embrace Your forgiveness because You died to set me free from a life of sin. I yield my life to You and I choose to live for You, all the days of my life.

I ask for Your precious Holy Spirit to come in and have His way in my life and in my future.

In Jesus' Mighty Name I pray.

If you just prayed this prayer, I congratulate you big time! Heaven is rejoicing at this very moment because of you.

Luke 15:7

Count on it--there's more joy in heaven over one sinner's rescued life than over ninety-nine good people in no need of rescue. (MSG)

The next step is to become planted in the service of the Lord, in any Bible believing church. For further counseling and prayers, please contact us at Watchmaidens Ministry, with the information on page 2 of the book; the copyright disclaimer page.

The world is waiting for you to rise out of spiritual dryness, and be a living evidence of God's experiential love. Start manifesting in Jesus' Mighty Name! Congratulations!

ABOUT THE AUTHOR

Watchmaidens Ministry is a Christian interdenominational Para – Church Mission organization, based in Lagos, Nigeria. Founded in September, 2011, Watchmaidens has a clear and strong intercessory mandate anchored on the Word of God, and the vision to pray for the body of Christ, "The Church", the Nations of the world, lost souls and the lost in the Church.

To the glory of God, we have thus far been empowered by the grace of God to stand in this intercessory assignment. Now the Lord has birthed yet another book, born out of a passion to see Christians who are stuck in spiritual dryness, and a lack of God's experiential love, restored to the original image of God. A Church without spot or wrinkle.

www.ingramcontent.com/pod-product-compliance
Lightning Source LLC
Chambersburg PA
CBHW071456040426
42444CB00008B/1360